United States
Department of
Agriculture

Forest
Service

Northern
Research Station

General Technical
Report
NRS-8

Bibliography of Forest Water Yields, Flooding Issues, and the Hydrologic Modeling of Extreme Flood Events

Mark H. Eisenbies, Mary Beth Adams, W. Michael Aust, and James A. Burger

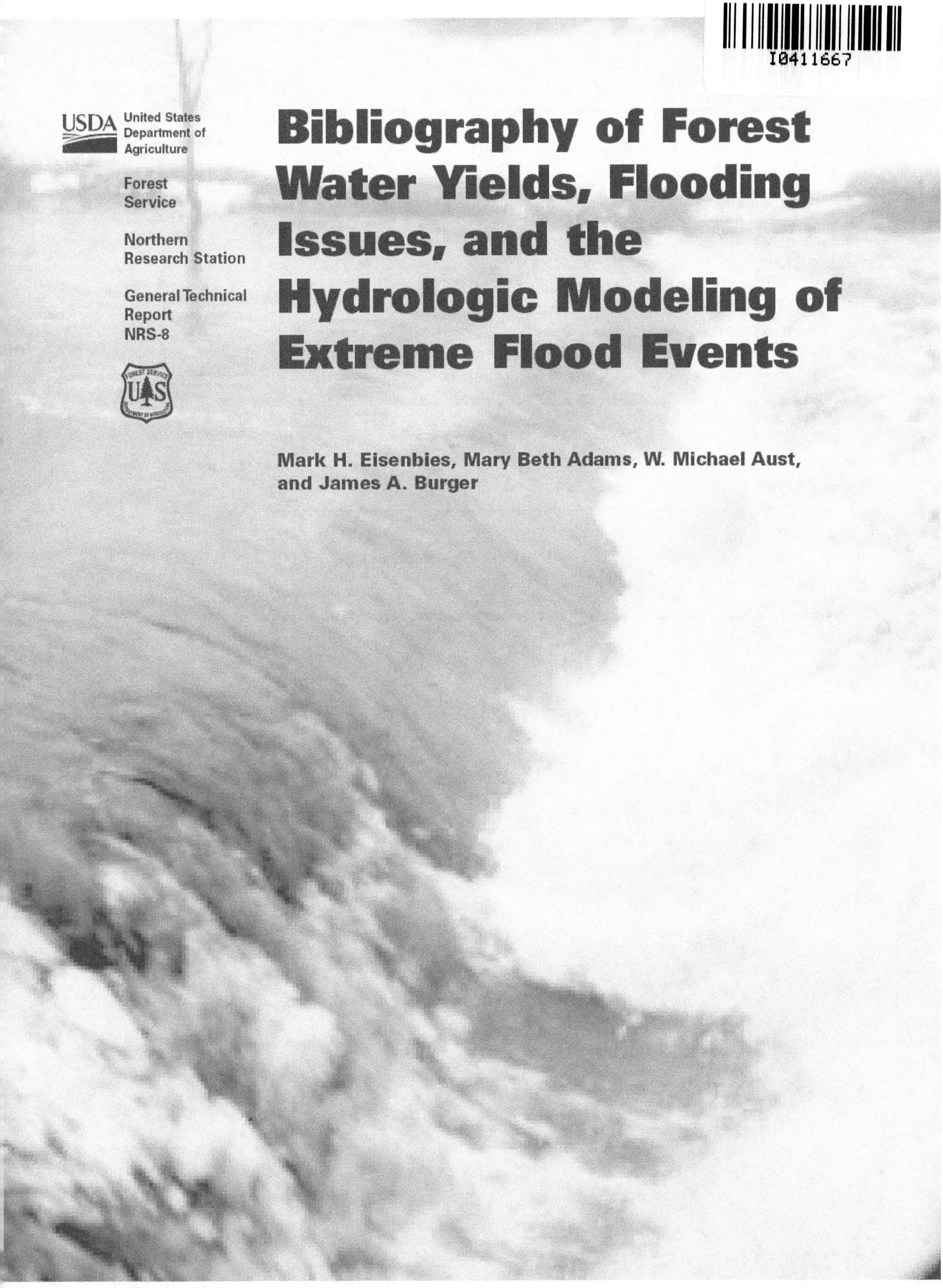

Abstract

Floods continue to cause significant damage in the United States and else-where, and questions about the causes of flooding continue to be debated. A significant amount of research has been conducted on the relationship between forest management activities and water yield, peak flows, and flooding; some-what less research has been conducted on the modeling of these activities as related to flooding. This bibliography and online bibliographic database provide a searchable listing of more than 600 publications related to the interrelationships of forest and forest management on watershed and flood hydrology. Also included are publications related to the capability and limitations of currently available hydrologic models and modeling approaches, with particular emphasis on their utility for evaluating forest management effects.

INTRODUCTION

The connection between forests and water resources is well established, but the relationships among the components are only partially understood. There is some evidence that the frequency of severe flooding may be on the rise due to climate change and permanent large-scale changes in land use (Macklin and Lewin 2003). Floods caused an estimated $90 billion in damage in the United States during the 1990s (Pielke et al. 2002), and recent severe flooding in the U.S. has renewed interest in the relationships among land use, forest management operations, and proportionate surface runoff. Recurrent flooding in the Appalachians has been especially troublesome and has resulted in extensive property damage and the loss of human lives.

Extreme rainstorms have the potential to cause considerable economic damage to persons and property, usually due to either flooding or landslides. The severity of these events can be influenced by numerous climatic and site factors such as rainfall amounts and intensity, existing soil moisture content, soil depth, slope, geographic aspect, and geology (glaciated versus unglaciated). Land use and management practices have also been identified as influential factors and are the only variables over which humans have any reasonable degree of control.

Because forested watersheds have been relied upon for centuries to protect water resources, land uses such as forestry, agriculture, urbanization, and mining have come under increasing scrutiny for their potential and perceived effects on water quality and quantity. Public and political pressure to prevent future floods usually follows large, damaging events, and forest protection is often a centerpiece of prevention plans. Such plans should be based upon the best available information, which of necessity comes from long-term research.

The U.S. has traditionally been very active in the area of forested watershed research. Between 1900 and 1950 about 150 watershed studies were conducted, primarily to assess the effects of land management on water yield (Stednick 1996). Several long-term research facilities in the Appalachian region are dedicated to basic research in forest hydrology (Adams et al. 2003). These facilities include the Coweeta Hydrologic Laboratory in North Carolina (est. 1934), the Fernow Experimental Forest in West Virginia (est. 1934), the Hubbard Brook Ecosystem Study in New Hampshire (est. 1962), and the Walker Branch Research Project in Tennessee (est. 1967). These facilities have each accumulated between 35 and 70 years of nearly continuous stream discharge and other data, which represent the best long-term datasets available in the Appalachian region. Research at these sites addresses a variety of large-scale and small-scale ecological questions; however, none of the sites were established expressly to research extreme flooding.

Nonetheless, a significant amount of knowledge about the links between forests and watershed hydrology has been gained in the Appalachian region. Cutting trees reduces water demand and can affect water yield from forested watersheds primarily during the growing season. Forest road systems may affect hillslope hydrology and flow routing to rivers and streams. Rapid subsequent runoff and increased water yield may in turn affect the frequency and magnitude of local and regional floods, but this remains to be demonstrated in the field. The influence of forestry practices and the specific mechanisms by which they affect flooding remain the focus of much research and debate throughout the world.

The Authors

MARK H. EISENBIES, Research Associate, College of Natural Resources, Virginia Tech. University, Blacksburg, VA.

M.B. ADAMS, Project Leader, Research Soil Scientist, USDA Forest Service, Northern Research Station, Parsons, WV.

W. MICHAEL AUST, Professor of Forestry, College of Natural Resources, Virginia Tech. University, Blacksburg, VA.

JAMES A. BURGER, Professor of Forestry, College of Natural Resources, Virginia Tech. University, Blacksburg, VA.

Despite centuries of scientific observations and research inspired by major flooding events, many aspects about the relationship between land use and flooding remain unresolved (Andreassian 2004). Extreme events are rare, and because of the complexity of the system and the cost of installing large-scale hydrologic studies, data are usually limited for answering specific research questions. Models are therefore frequently used to simulate reality in comparing and evaluating land use scenarios or to reconstruct floods after they occur.

The Bibliography

We created this bibliography to provide an extensive listing of available literature on the interrelationships of forests and forest management on watershed and flood hydrology. Also provided is a listing of literature on the capability and limitations of currently available hydrologic models and modeling approaches for evaluating the effects of land use on flooding. At the time of publication, this bibliography includes a total of 617 citations that are cross-listed within 12 general categories as they relate to land use, hydrology, flooding, and modeling; individual citations may appear in multiple categories. Some emphasis has been placed on articles concerning extreme flooding and the Appalachian region. Citations after 1980 are emphasized and are primarily drawn from journal articles, books, and book chapters (fig. 1). Proceedings papers, reports, and other items are included based on their relative availability.

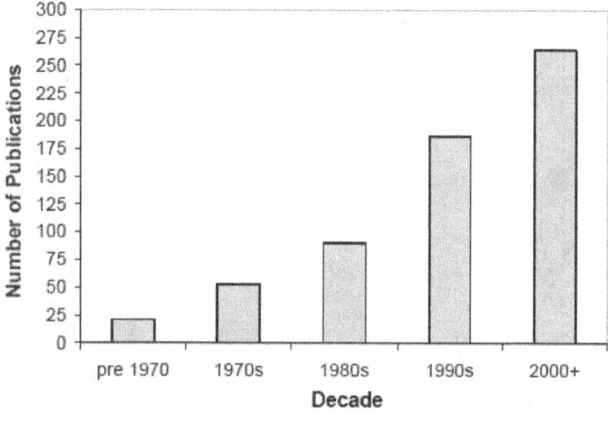

Figure 1.—*Number of publications cited in this document corresponding to decade.*

Category Descriptions

(1) *Forest hydrology, policy, history, case studies, and watershed function:* a broad overview of forest hydrology as well as case studies of specific floods.

(2) *Watersheds, forest, and hillslope hydrology:* general hydrologic concepts concerning the water cycle.

(3) *Geomorphology:* stream and flood topography, geomorphology, and fluvial processes.

(4) *Forest operations and management effects:* silvicultural and harvesting effects on hydrology and soils.

(5) *Nonforest land use effects:* impacts of other land uses (agriculture, mining, and urban) on hydrology and soils.

(6) *Soil disturbance, roads, and best management practices:* soil disturbance effects on hydrology and management implications and prescriptions for reducing erosion and protecting water quality.

(7) *Modeling approaches, concepts, and reviews:* general techniques and a variety of models for simulating hydrology on watersheds.

(8) *Hydrologic model descriptions and applications:* specific application of models.

(9) *Land use hydrologic modeling:* models specifically designed to evaluate land use change.

(10) *Hillslope hydrologic modeling:* models designed for hillslope hydrology.

(11) *Modeling issues:* a wide variety of modeling issues including uncertainty, scale, heterogeneity, thresholds, and inference.

(12) *Flood frequency analysis:* techniques for determining the return periods of floods and rain events.

Using This Bibliography

This bibliography is available at
http://www.nrs.fs.fed.us/flooding as a printed document,
searchable online database, or as a downloadable
EndNote™ database[1]. The information will be updated
periodically, and we encourage readers to send additional citations and reprints for inclusion in the updates (see
the Web site above for more information). Most of these
references may be obtained from public or university
libraries directly or via interlibrary loan. Reports are
usually available from the publishing agency.

Literature Cited

Adams, M.B.; Loughry, L.H.; Plaugher, L.L. 2003.
**Experimental forests and ranges of the USDA
Forest Service.** Gen. Tech. Rep. NE-321. Newtown
Square, PA: U.S. Department of Agriculture, Forest
Service, Northeastern Research Station. 178 p.

Andreassian, V. 2004. **Waters and forests: from historical controversy to scientific debate.** Journal of
Hydrology. 291(1-2): 1-27.

Macklin, M.G.; Lewin, J. 2003. **River sediments, great
floods and centennial-scale Holocene climate
change.** Journal of Quaternary Science. 18: 101-105.

Pielke, R.A., Jr.; Downton, M.W.; Miller, J.Z.B. 2002.
**Flood damage in the United States, 1926-2000: a
reanalysis of National Weather Service estimates.**
Boulder, CO: National Center for Atmospheric
Research. 96 p.

Stednick, J.D. 1996. **Monitoring the effects of timber
harvest on annual water yield.** Journal of
Hydrology. 176: 79-95.

Forest Hydrology, Policy, History, Case Studies, and Watershed Function

Adams, M.B.; Loughry, L.H.; Plaugher, L.L. 2003.
**Experimental forests and ranges of the USDA
Forest Service.** Gen. Tech. Rep. NE-321. Newtown
Square, PA: U.S. Department of Agriculture, Forest
Service, Northeastern Research Station. 178 p.

---

[1] *Mention of product or trade names does not constitute
endorsement by the USDA Forest Service.*

Adams, M.B.; Kochenderfer, J.N.; Wood, F.; Angradi,
T.R.; Edwards, P. 1994. **Forty years of hydrometeo-
rological data from the Fernow Experimental
Forest, West Virginia.** Gen. Tech. Rep. NE-184.
Radnor, PA: U.S. Department of Agriculture, Forest
Service, Northeastern Forest Experiment Station.
24 p.

Adams, P.W. 1993. **Closing the gaps in knowledge,
policy and action to address water issues in
forests.** Journal of Hydrology. 150: 773-786.

Andreassian, V. 2004. **Waters and forests: from historical controversy to scientific debate.** Journal of
Hydrology. 291: 1-27.

Bates, C.G.; Henry, A.J. 1928. **Forest and streamflow
experiment at Wagon Wheel Gap, Colorado.**
Monthly Weather Review, Suppl. 30. Washington,
DC: U.S. Weather Bureau. 79 p.

Benson, M.A. 1960. **Characteristics of frequency
curves based on a theoretical 1000-year record.**
In: Dalrymple, T., ed. Flood frequency analyses.
Water-Supply Pap. 1543. U.S. Geological Survey.:
51-74.

Black, P.E. 1996. **Watershed hydrology.** 2d ed. New
York: Lewis. 450 p.

Black, P.E. 2004. **Forest and wildland watershed func-
tions.** In: Ice, G.G.; Stednick, J.D., eds. A century of
forest and wildland watershed lessons. Bethesda,
MD: Society of American Foresters: 1-18.

Boyd, L.; MacNally, R.; Read, J. 2005. **Does fallen timber on floodplains influence distribution of nutri-
ents, plants, and seeds?** Plant Ecology. 177: 165-
176.

Brissette, F.P.; Leconte, R.; Marche, C.; Rousselle, J.
2003. **Historical evolution of flooding damage on
a USA/Quebec River Basin.** Journal of the American
Water Resources Association. 39: 1385-1396.

Bruins, R.J.F.; Shuming, C.; Shijian, C.; Mitsch, W.J.
1998. **Ecological engineering strategies to reduce
flooding damage to wetland crops in central
China.** Ecological Engineering. 11: 231-259.

Brzozowski, C. 2004. **A flood of concern in Roanoke.** American Forests. 110: 38-43.

Calder, I.R. 2006. **Forest and floods: moving to an evidence-based approach to watershed and integrated flood management.** Water International. 31: 87-99.

Chang, M. 2006. **Forest hydrology.** 2d ed. New York: CRC Press. 474 p.

Dalton, R. 2005. **Floods fail to save canyon beaches.** Nature. 438: 10.

DeBano, L.F.; Rice, R.M. 1973. **Water repellent soils: their implication in forestry.** Journal of Forestry. 71: 220-223.

DeWalle, D.R. 2003. **Forest hydrology revisited.** Hydrological Processes. 17: 1255-1256.

Eyre, F.H., ed. 1980. **Forest cover types of the United States and Canada.** Washington, DC: Society of American Foresters. 148 p.

FAO, CIFOR. 2005. **Forests and floods: drowning in fiction or thriving in facts?** Bangkok, Thailand: U.N. Food and Agriculture Organization, Center for International Forestry Research. 40 p.

FATT. 2002. **Runoff analysis of Seng, Scrabble, and Sycamore Creeks.** Charleston, WV: Flood Advisory Technical Team. 123 p.

Fisher, R.F.; Binkley, D. 2000. **Ecology and management of forest soils.** 3d ed. New York: Wiley & Sons. 489 p.

Gaume, E.; Livet, M.; Desbordes, M. 2003. **Study of the hydrological processes during the Avene river extraordinary flood (south of France): 6-7 October 1997.** Physics and Chemistry of the Earth. 28: 263-267.

Gaume, E.; Livet, M.; Desbordes, M.; Villeneuve, J.-P. 2004. **Hydrological analysis of the river Aude, France, flash flood on 12 and 13 November 1999.** Journal of Hydrology. 286: 135-154.

Giordano, L.A.; Fritsch, J.M. 1991. **Strong tornados and flash-flood-producing rainstorms during the warm season in the Mid-Atlantic Region.** Weather and Forecasting. 6: 437-455.

Hack, J.T.; Goodlett, J.C. 1960. **Geomorphology and forest ecology of a mountain region in the central Appalachians.** U.S. Geological Surv. Prof. Pap. 347. Washington, DC: U.S. Government Printing Office. 66 p.

Holman, I.P.; Hollis, J.M.; Bramley, M.E.; Thompson, T.R.E. 2003. **The contribution of soil structural degradation to catchment flooding: a preliminary investigation of the 2000 floods in England and Wales.** Hydrology and Earth System Sciences. 7: 754-765.

Hursh, C.R. 1951. **Watershed aspects of the New York water supply problems.** Journal of Forestry. 49: 442-444.

Keller, H.M. 1988. **European experiences in long-term forest hydrology research.** In: Swank, W.T.; Crossley, D.A., Jr., eds. Forest hydrology and ecology at Coweeta. New York: Springer-Verlag: 407-414.

Lee, R. 1980. **Forest hydrology.** New York: Columbia University Press. 349 p.

Lu, S.-Y.; Cheng, J.D.; Brooks, K.N. 2001. **Managing forests for watershed protection in Taiwan.** Forest Ecology and Management. 143: 77-85.

Lull, H.W.; Reinhart, K.G. 1972. **Forests and floods.** Res. Pap. NE-226. Upper Darby, PA: U.S. Department of Agriculture, Forest Service, Northeastern Forest Experiment Station. 94 p.

Macklin, M.G.; Lewin, J. 2003. **River sediments, great floods and centennial-scale Holocene climate change.** Journal of Quaternary Science. 18: 101-105.

McCulloch, J.; Robinson, M. 1993. **History of forest hydrology.** Journal of Hydrology. 150: 189-216.

McDonald, B.R.; Trianosky, P. 1995. **Assessment of, and management recommendations for, the plant communities and rare species of Camp Brookside,**

New River Gorge National River. Tech. Rep. 95-5. Elkins, WV: West Virginia Natural Heritage Program. 24 p.

Miller, J.B. 1997. **Floods - people at risk, strategies for prevention.** New York and Geneva: United Nations, Department of Humanitarian Affairs. 93 p.

Mortimer, M.J.; Visser, R.J.M. 2004. **Timber harvesting and flooding: emerging legal risks and potential mitigations.** Southern Journal of Applied Forestry. 28: 69-75.

Newson, M.D. 1975. **Flooding and flood hazard in the United Kingdom.** Oxford, England: Oxford University Press. 60 p.

NYDEP. 2005. **New York City's water supply system: history.** New York Department of Environmental Protection. http://www.nyc.gov/html/dep/html/history.html. Last updated January 17, 2007.

Olshansky, R.B.; Rogers, J.D. 1992. **The concept of 'reasonable care' on unstable hillsides.** In: Slosson, J.E.; et al., eds. Reviews in engineering geology - landslides/landslide mitigation. Boulder, CO: Geological Society of America: 9: 23-27.

Patric, J.H.; Kidd, W.E.J. 1982. **Erosion on very stony forest soil during phenomenal rain in Webster County, West Virginia.** Res. Pap. NE-501. Upper Darby, PA: U.S. Department of Agriculture, Forest Service, Northeastern Forest Experiment Station. 13 p.

Patten, D.T.; Stevens, L.E. 2001. **Restoration of the Colorado River ecosystem using planned flooding.** Ecological Applications. 11: 633-634.

Patten, D.T.; Harpman, D.A.; Voita, M.I.; Randle, T.J. 2001. **A managed flood on the Colorado River: background, objectives, design, and implementation.** Ecological Applications. 11: 635-643.

Perry, C.A.; Combs, L.J. 1998. **Summary of floods in the United States, January 1992 through September 1993.** Water-Supply Pap. 2499. Denver, CO: U.S. Geological Survey. [http://ks.water.usgs.gov/Kansas/pubs/reports/wsp.2499.html] (15 September 2005).

Pielke, R.A., Jr.; Downton, M.W.; Miller, J.Z.B. 2002. **Flood damage in the United States, 1926-2000: a reanalysis of National Weather Service estimates.** Boulder, CO: National Center for Atmospheric Research. 96 p.

Pritchett, W.L.; Fisher, R.F. 1987. **Properties and management of forest soils.** 2d ed. New York: Wiley & Sons. 494 p.

Rouse, G.D.; McDonald, B.R. 1986. **Rare vascular plant survey - New River Gorge National River.** Res. Resour. Manage. Rep. CA-4000-4-0012. Philadelphia, PA: U.S. Department of the Interior, National Park Service. 55 p.

Ryan, P.J.; Hornbeck, J.W. 2004. **Watersheds.** Wildland Waters. Spring 2004: 2-16.

Stevens, L.E.; Ayers, T.J.; Bennett, J.B.; Christensen, K.; Kearsley, M.J.C.; Meretsky, V.J.; Phillips, A.M.; Parnell, R.A.; Spence, J.; Sogge, M.K.; Springer, A.E.; Wegner, D.L. 2001. **Planned flooding and Colorado River riparian trade-offs downstream from Glen Canyon Dam, Arizona.** Ecological Applications. 11: 701-710.

Swanson, R.H. 1998. **Forest hydrology issues for the 21st century: a consultant's viewpoint.** Journal of the American Water Resources Division. 34: 755-763.

Troch, P.A.; Smith, C.T.; Wood, E.F.; DeTroch, F.P. 1994. **Hydrologic controls of large floods in a small basin: central Appalachian case study.** Journal of Hydrology. 156: 285-309.

Twery, M.J.; Hornbeck, J.W. 2001. **Incorporating water goals into forest management at a local level.** Forest Ecology and Management. 143: 87-93.

USGS. 2003. **Physiographic regions.** U.S. Geological Survey. http://tapestry.usgs.gov/physiogr/physio.html] (22 December 2005).

Wear, D.N.; Bolstad, P.V. 1998. **Land-use changes in southern Appalachian landscapes: special analysis and forecast evaluation.** Ecosystems. 1: 575-594.

Wear, D.N.; Turner, M.G.; Flamm, R.O. 1996. **Ecosystem management with multiple owners: landscape dynamics in a southern Appalachian watershed.** Ecological Applications. 6: 1173-1188.

Williams, H. 1978. **Tectonic-Lithofacies map of the Appalachian Orogen.** Map No. 1, 1:1,000,000 scale. St. John's, Newfoundland, Canada: Memorial University of Newfoundland.

Yeo, S.W. 2002. **Flooding in Australia: a review of events in 1998.** Natural Hazards. 25: 177-191.

Watersheds, Forest, and Hillslope Hydrology

Abdul, A.S.; Gillham, R.W. 1984. **Laboratory studies of the effects of the capillary fringe on streamflow generation.** Water Resources Research. 20: 691-698.

Allan, J.D.; Johnson, L.B. 1997. **Catchment-scale analysis of aquatic ecosystems.** Freshwater Biology. 37: 107-111.

Anderson, S.P.; Dietrich, W.E.; Torres, R. 1997. **Concentration-discharge relationships in runoff from a steep, unchanneled catchment.** Water Resources Research. 33: 211-225.

Anderson, S.P.; Dietrich, W.E.; Montgomery, D.R.; Torres, R.; Conrad, M.E.; Loague, K. 1997. **Subsurface flow paths in a steep, unchanneled catchment.** Water Resources Research. 33: 2637-2653.

Band, L.E.; Patterson, P.; Ramakrishna, N.; Running, S.W. 1993. **Forest ecosystem processes at the watershed scale: incorporating hillslope hydrology.** Agricultural and Forest Meteorology. 63: 93-126.

Band, L.E.; Tague, C.; Groffman, P.; Belt, K. 2001. **Forest ecosystem processes at the watershed scale: hydrological and ecological controls of nitrogen export.** Hydrological Processes. 15: 2013-2028.

Bazemore, D.E.; Eshleman, K.N.; Hollenbeck, K.J. 1994. **The role of soil water in stormflow generation in** a forested headwater catchment: synthesis of natural tracer and hydrometric evidence. Journal of Hydrology. 162: 47-75.

Benda, L.E.; Andras, K.; Miller, D.; Bigelow, P. 2004. **Confluence effects in rivers: interactions of basin scale, network geometry, and disturbance regimes.** Water Resources Research. 40: 1-15.

Beven, K.J.; Germann, P. 1982. **Macropores and water flow in soils.** Water Resources Research. 18: 1311-1325.

Black, P.E. 1972. **Hydrograph responses to geomorphic model watershed characteristics and precipitation variables.** Journal of Hydrology. 17: 309-329.

Black, P.E. 1996. **Watershed hydrology.** 2d ed. New York: Lewis. 450 p.

Bonell, M. 1993. **Progress in the understanding of runoff generation dynamics in forests.** Journal of Hydrology. 150: 217-275.

Bonell, M. 1998. **Selected challenges in runoff generation research in forests from the hillslope to headwater drainage basin scale.** Journal of the American Water Resources Division. 34: 765-785.

Bren, L.J. 1993. **Riparian zone, stream, and floodplain issues: a review.** Journal of Hydrology. 150: 277-299.

Brooks, K.N.; Ffolliott, P.F.; Gregersen, H.M.; DeBano, L.F. 2003. **Hydrology and the management of watersheds.** 3d ed. Ames, IA: Iowa State Press. 574 p.

Brutsaert, W. 2005. **Hydrology: an introduction.** New York: Cambridge University Press. 618 p.

Buttle, J.M.; Metcalfe, R.A. 2000. **Boreal forest disturbance and streamflow response, northeastern Ontario.** Canadian Journal of Fisheries and Aquatic Sciences. 57: 5-18.

Buttle, J.M.; Hazlett, P.W.; Murray, C.D.; Creed, I.F.; Jeffries, D.S.; Semkin, R. 2001. **Prediction of** groundwater characteristics in forested and harvested basins during spring snowmelt using a topographic index. Hydrological Processes. 15: 3389-3407.

Carter, B.J.; Ciolkosz, E.J. 1991. **Slope gradient and aspect effects on soils developed from sandstone in Pennsylvania.** Geoderma. 49: 199-213.

Casper, M.C.; Volkmann, H.N.; Waldenmeyer, G.; Plate, E.J. 2003. **The separation of flow pathways in a sandstone catchment of the Northern Black Forest using DOC and a nested approach.** Physics and Chemistry of the Earth. 28: 269-275.

Crawford, N.C. 1982. **Karst hydrology of Tennessee.** Washington, DC: U.S. Environmental Protection Agency. 102 p.

Curry, R.A.; Scruton, D.A.; Clarke, K.D. 2002. **The thermal regimes of brook trout incubation habitats and evidence of changes during forestry operations.** Canadian Journal of Forest Research. 32: 1200-1207.

Dunne, T.; Black, R.D. 1970a. **An experimental investigation of runoff production in permeable soils.** Water Resources Research. 6: 478-490.

Dunne, T.; Black, R.D. 1970b. **Partial area contributions to storm runoff in a small New England watershed.** Water Resources Research. 6: 1296-1311.

Dykes, A.P.; Thornes, J.B. 2000. **Hillslope hydrology in tropical rainforest steeplands in Brunei.** Hydrological Processes. 14: 215-235.

Freeze, R.A.; Cherry, J.A. 1979. **Groundwater hydrology.** Edgewood Cliffs, NJ: Prentice Hall. 604 p.

Gburek, W.J.; Folmar, G.J. 1999. **Flow and chemical contributions to streamflow in an upland watershed: a baseflow survey.** Journal of Hydrology. 217: 1-18.

Genereux, D.P.; Hemond, H.F.; Mulholland, P.J. 1993. **Use of radon-222 and calcium as tracers in a three-end-member mixing model for streamflow generation on the West Fork of Walker Branch Watershed.** Journal of Hydrology. 142: 167-211.

Godsey, S.; Elsenbeer, H. 2002. **The soil hydrologic response to forest regrowth: a case study from southwestern Amazonia.** Hydrological Processes. 16: 1519-1522.

Gomi, T.; Sidle, R.C.; Richardson, J.S. 2002. **Understanding processes and downstream linkages of headwater systems.** BioScience. 52: 905-916.

Guebert, M.D.; Gardner, T.W. 2001. **Macropore flow on a reclaimed surface mine: infiltration and hillslope hydrology.** Geomorphology. 39: 151-169.

Hammermeister, D.P.; Kling, G.F.; Vomocil, J.A. 1982a. **Perched water tables on hillsides in western Oregon: I. Some factors affecting their development and longevity.** Soil Science Society of America Journal. 46: 811-818.

Hammermeister, D.P.; Kling, G.F.; Vomocil, J.A. 1982b. **Perched water tables on hillsides in western Oregon: II. Preferential downslope movement of water and anions.** Soil Science Society of America Journal. 46: 819-826.

Heilig, A.; Steenhuis, T.A.; Walter, M.T.; Herbert, S.J. 2003. **Funneled flow mechanisms in layered soil: field investigations.** Journal of Hydrology. 279: 210-223.

Hess, J.W.; White, W.B. 1989. **Water budget and physical hydrology.** In: White, W.B.; White, E.L., eds. Karst hydrology—concepts from the Mammoth Cave area. New York: Van Nostrand Reinhold: 105-126.

Hewlett, J.D. 1961. **Soil moisture as a source of base flow from steep mountain watersheds.** Pap. 132. Asheville, NC: U.S. Department of Agriculture, Forest Service, Southeastern Forest Experiment Station. 11 p.

Hewlett, J.D. 1982. **Principles of forest hydrology.** Athens, GA: University of Georgia Press. 192 p.

Hewlett, J.D.; Fortson, J.C.; Cunningham, G.B. 1984. **Additional tests on the effect of rainfall intensity** on storm flow and peak flow from wild-land basins. Water Resources Research. 20: 985-989.

Hibbert, A.D. 1967. **Forest treatment effects on water yield.** In: Sopper, W.E.; Lull, H.W., eds. Forest hydrology: proceedings of a National Science Foundation advanced science seminar; 1965 August 29-September 10; University Park, PA. Oxford, England: Pergamon Press: 527-543.

Hill, A.R.; Waddington, J.M. 1993. **Analysis of storm run-off sources using oxygen-18 in a headwater swamp.** Hydrological Processes. 7: 305-316.

Hillel, D. 1982. **Introduction to soil physics.** New York: Academic Press. 365 p.

Huff, D.D.; O'Neill, R.V.; Emanuel, W.R.; Elwood, J.W.; Newbold, J.D. 1982. **Flow variability and hillslope hydrology.** Earth Surface Processes and Landforms. 7: 91-94.

Hursh, C.R. 1936. **Storm water and adsorption.** Eos Transactions, American Geophysical Union, Part 2: 301-302.

Jayasuriya, M.D.A.; Dunn, G.; Benyon, R.; O'Shaughnessy, P.J. 1993. **Some factors affecting water yield from mountain ash (*Eucalyptus regnans*) dominated forests in southeast Australia.** Journal of Hydrology. 150: 345-367.

Johnson, R. 1998. **The forest cycle and low river flows: a review of UK and international studies.** Forest Ecology and Management. 109: 1-7.

Lee, R. 1970. **Theoretical estimates versus forest water yield.** Water Resources Research. 6: 1327-1334.

Legrand, H.E.; Stringfield, V.T. 1973. **Karst hydrology - a review.** Journal of Hydrology. 20: 97-120.

Lockaby, B.G.; Clawson, R.G.; Flynn, K.; Rummer, R.; Meadows, S.; Stokes, B.; Stanturf, J. 1997. **Influence of harvesting on biogeochemical exchange in sheetflow and soil processes in a eutrophic floodplain forest.** Forest Ecology and Management. 90: 187-194.

Lotspeich, F.B. 1980. **Watersheds as the basic ecosystem: this conceptual framework provides a basis for a natural classification system.** Water Resources Bulletin. 16: 581-586.

Lull, H.W.; Reinhart, K.G. 1972. **Forests and floods.** Res. Pap. NE-226. Upper Darby, PA: U.S. Department of Agriculture, Forest Service, Northeastern Forest Experiment Station. 94 p.

Luxmoore, R.J. 1981. **Micro-, meso-, and macroporosity of soil.** Soil Science Society of America Journal. 45: 671.

Luxmoore, R.J.; Huff, D.D. 1989. **Water.** In: Johnson, D.; Van Hook, R.I., eds. Analysis of biogeochemical cycling processes in Walker Branch Watershed. New York: Springer-Verlag: 164-196.

Luxmoore, R.J.; Jardine, P.M.; Wilson, G.V.; Jones, J.R.; Zelazny, L.W. 1990. **Physical and chemical controls of preferred path flow through a forested hillslope.** Geoderma. 46: 139-154.

McCulloch, J.; Robinson, M. 1993. **History of forest hydrology.** Journal of Hydrology. 150: 189-216.

McNabb, D.H.; Gaweda, F.; Froehlich, H.A. 1989. **Infiltration, water repellency, and soil moisture content after broadcast burning a forest site in southwest Oregon.** Water Resources Research. 24: 155-162.

Meng, F.; Bourque, C.; Jewett, K.; Daugharty, D.; Arp, P. 1995. **The Nashwaak Experimental Watershed Project: analysing effects of clearcutting on soil temperature, soil moisture, snowpack, snowmelt, and stream flow.** Water, Air, and Soil Pollution. 82: 363-374.

Mulholland, P.J. 1993. **Hydrometric and stream chemistry evidence of three stormpaths in Walker Branch Watershed.** Journal of Hydrology. 151: 291-316.

Mulholland, P.J.; Wilson, G.V.; Jardine, P.M. 1990. **Hydrogeochemical response of a forested watershed to storms: effects of preferential flow along shallow and deep pathways.** Water Resources Research. 26: 3021-3036.

Neatraour, M.A.; Webster, J.R.; Benfield, E.F. 2004. The role of floods in particulate organic matter dynamics of a southern Appalachian river-flood-plain ecosystem. Journal of the North American Benthological Society 23 198-213.

Newson, M.D. 1975. Flooding and flood hazard in the United Kingdom. Oxford, England Oxford University Press 60 p.

Pearce, A.J.; Stewart, M.K.; Sklash, M.G. 1986. Storm runoff generation in humid headwa er catchments 1: Where does the water come from? Water Resources Research. 2 : 1263-1272.

Philip, J R 1969 Theory of infiltration. In: Chow, V.T., ed Advances in hydrosciences. New York Academic Press: 5: 215-291

Pilgrim, D.H.; Cordery, I. 1993. Flood runoff. In: Maidment, D.R., ed. Handbook of hydrology. New York: McGraw-Hill: 9 1-42.

Riverbark, B L ; Jackson, C.R 2004a. Average discharge, perennial flow initiation, and channel initiation - small Southern Appalachian basins. Journal of the American Water Resources Association. 40: 639-646.

Riverbark, B L.; Jackson, C.R. 2004b. Concentrated flow breakthroughs moving through silvicultural streamside management zones: Southeastern Piedmont, USA. Journal of the American Water Resources Association 40: 1043-1052

Robinson, M.; Cognard-Plancq, A.-L.; Cosandey, C.; David, J.; Durand, P.; Fuhrer, H.-W.; Hall, R.; Hendriques, M.O ; Marc, V.; McCarthy, R.; McDonnell, M.; Martin, C W.; Nisbet, T.; O'Dea, P.; Rogers, M.; Zollner, A. 2003. Studies on the impact of forests on peak flows and baseflows: a European perspective. Forest Ecology and Management. 186: 85-97.

Ruprecht, J.K.; Stoneman, G.L. 1993. Water yield issues in the jarrah forest of southwestern Australia. Journal of Hydrology. 150: 369-391.

Sherlock, M.D ; McDonnell, J.J. 2003. A new tool for hillslope hydrologists: spatially distributed groundwater level and soil water content measured using electromagnetic induction Hydrological Processes 17: 1965 977

Shuttleworth, W.J. 1993. Evaporation. In: Maidment, D.R , ed Handbook of hydr logy. New York: McGraw-Hill 4 1-53

Sidle, R.C.; Kitahara, H.; Terajima, T.; Nakai, Y. 1995. Experimental studies on the effects of pipeflow on throughflow partitioning. Journal of Hydrology. 165: 207-219

Sidle, R.C.; Noguchi, S.; Tsuboyama, Y.; Laursen, K. 2001 A conceptual model of preferential flow systems in forested hillslopes: evidence of self organization. Hydrological Processes. 15: 1675-1692.

Sidle, R.C ; Tsuboyama, Y.; Noguchi, S.; Hosoda, I.; Fujieda, M ; Shimizu, T 1995. Seasonal hydrologic response at various spatial scales in a small forested catchment, Hitachi Ohta, Japan. Journal of Hydrology. 168: 227-250.

Sidle, R.C.; Tsuboyama, Y.; Noguchi, S.; Hosoda, I.; Fujieda, M.; Shimizu, T. 2000. Stormflow generation in steep forested headwaters: a linked hydro-geomo phic paradigm Hydrological Processes 14: 369-385

Smith, R.E.; Woolhiser, D.A. 1971. Overland flow on an infilt ating surface. Water Resources Research. 7: 899-913.

Swanson, R H. 1998. Forest hydrology issues for the 21st century: a consultant's viewpoint. Journal of the American Water Resources Division 34: 755-763.

Swift, L.W.; Cunningham, G.B.; Douglass, J.E. 1988. Climatology and hydrology. In: Swank, W.T.; Crossley, D.A., Jr., eds. Forest hydrology and ecology at Coweeta. New York: Springer-Verlag: 35-56.

Torres, R. 2002. A threshold condition for soil-water transport. Hydrological Processes. 16: 2703-2706.

Torres, R.; Alexander, L.J. 2002. **Intensity-duration effects on drainage: column experiments at near-zero pressure head.** Water Resources Research. 38: 1-10.

Torres, R.; Dietrich, W.E.; Montgomery, D.R.; Anderson, S.P.; Loague, K. 1998. **Unsaturated zone processes and the hydrologic response of a steep, unchanneled catchment.** Water Resources Research. 34: 1865-1879.

Tsuboyama, Y.; Sidle, R.C.; Noguchi, S.; Murakami, S.; Shimizu, T. 2000. **A zero-order basin – its contribution to catchment hydrology and internal hydrological processes.** Hydrological Processes. 14: 387-401.

Tsukamoto, Y.; Ohta, T. 1988. **Runoff process on a steep forested slope.** Journal of Hydrology. 102: 165-178.

Vachaud, G.; Thony, J.-L. 1971. **Hysteresis during infiltration and redistribution of a soil column at different initial water contents.** Water Resources Research. 7: 111-127.

Vertessy, R.A.; Watson, F.G.R.; O'Sullivan, S.K. 2001. **Factors determining relations between stand age and catchment water balance in mountain ash forests.** Forest Ecology and Management. 143: 13-26.

Waddington, J.M.; Roulet, N.T.; Hill, A.R. 1993. **Runoff mechanisms in a forested groundwater discharge wetland.** Journal of Hydrology. 147: 37-60.

Wei, X.; Liu, S.; Zhou, G.; Wang, C. 2005. **Hydrological processes in major types of Chinese forest.** Hydrological Processes. 19: 63-75.

Wels, C.; Cornett, R.J.; Lazerte, B.D. 1991. **Hydrograph separation: a comparison of geochemical and isotopic tracers.** Journal of Hydrology. 122: 253-274.

Weyman, D.R. 1973. **Measurements of the downslope flow of water in a soil.** Journal of Hydrology. 20: 267-288.

Whipkey, R.Z. 1965. **Subsurface stormflow from forested slopes.** Bulletin of the International Association of Scientific Hydrology. 10: 74-85.

White, E.L. 1989. **Flood hydrology.** In: White, W.B.; White, E.L., eds. Karst hydrology - concepts from the Mammoth Cave area. New York: Van Nostrand Reinhold: 127-143.

White, W.B.; White, E.L., eds. 1989. **Karst hydrology - concepts from the Mammoth Cave area.** New York: Van Nostrand Reinhold. 346 p.

Wilson, G.V.; Luxmoore, R.J. 1988. **Infiltration, macroporosity, and mesoporosity distribution on two forested watersheds.** Soil Science Society of America Journal. 52: 329-335.

Wilson, G.V.; Jardine, P.M.; Luxmoore, R.J.; Jones, J.R. 1990. **Hydrology of a forested hillslope during storm events.** Geoderma. 46: 119-138.

Wilson, G.V.; Jardine, P.M.; Luxmoore, R.J.; Zelazny, L.W.; Lietzke, D.A.; Todd, D.E. 1991a. **Hydrogeochemical processes controlling subsurface transport from an upper subcatchment of Walker Branch Watershed during storm events. 1: Hydrologic transport processes.** Journal of Hydrology. 123: 297-316.

Wilson, G.V.; Jardine, P.M.; Luxmoore, R.J.; Zelazny, L.W.; Todd, D.E.; Lietzke, D.A. 1991b. **Hydrogeochemical processes controlling subsurface transport from an upper subcatchment of Walker Branch Watershed during storm events. 2: Solute transport processes.** Journal of Hydrology. 123: 317-336.

Wilson, L.G.; Everett, L.G.; Cullen, S.J. 1995. **Handbook of vadose zone characterization and monitoring.** New York: Lewis. 750 p.

Winter, T.C. 1981. **Uncertainties in estimating the water balance of lakes.** Water Resources Bulletin. 17: 82-115.

Woodruff, J.F.; Hewlett, J.D. 1970. **Predicting and mapping the average hydrologic response for the Eastern United States.** Water Resources Research. 6: 1312-1326.

Wullschleger, S.D.; Meinzer, F.C.; Vertessy, R.A. 1998. **A review of whole-plant water use studies in trees.** Tree Physiology. 18: 499-512.

Zhang, X.; Ewen, J. 2000. **Efficient method for simulating gravity-dominated water flow in unsaturated soils.** Water Resources Research. 36: 2777-2780.

Geomorphology

Beebe, J. 2001. **Flow disturbance caused by cross-stream coarse woody debris.** Physical Geography. 22: 222-236.

Benda, L.E.; Andras, K.; Miller, D.; Bigelow, P. 2004. **Confluence effects in rivers: interactions of basin scale, network geometry, and disturbance regimes.** Water Resources Research. 40: 1-15.

Benda, L.E.; Hassan, M.A.; Church, M.; May, C.L. 2005. **Geomorphology of steepland headwaters: the transition from hillslopes to channels.** Journal of the American Water Resources Association. 41: 835-851.

Black, P.E. 1972. **Hydrograph responses to geomorphic model watershed characteristics and precipitation variables.** Journal of Hydrology. 17: 309-329.

Brooks, A.P.; Gehrke, P.C.; Jansen, J.D.; Abbe, T.B. 2004. **Experimental reintroduction of woody debris on the Williams River, NSW: geomorphic and ecological responses.** River Research and Applications. 20: 513-536.

Brown, D.A. 1971. **Stream channels and flow relations.** Water Resources Research. 7(2): 304-310.

Cammeraat, L.H. 2002. **A review of two strongly contrasting geomorphological systems within the context of scale.** Earth Surface Processes and Landforms. 27: 1201-1222.

Carter, B.J.; Ciolkosz, E.J. 1991. **Slope gradient and aspect effects on soils developed from sandstone in Pennsylvania.** Geoderma. 49: 199-213.

Clark, G.M. 1987. **Debris slide and debris flow historical events in the Appalachians south of the glacial border.** In: Costa, J.E.; Wieczorek, G.F., eds. Reviews in engineering geology - debris flows/avalanches: process, recognition, and mitigation. Boulder, CO: Geological Society of America: 7: 125-138.

Clark, J.J.; Wilcock, P.R. 2000. **Effects of land-use change on channel morphology in northeastern Puerto Rico.** Geological Society of America Bulletin. 112: 1763-1777.

Costa, J.E.; Miller, A.J.; Potter, K.W.; Wilcock, P.R., eds. 1995. **Natural and anthropogenic influences in fluvial geomorphology.** Geophys. Monogr. 89. Washington, DC: American Geophysical Union. 239 p.

Coulthard, T.J.; Kirkby, M.J.; Macklin, M.G. 2000. **Modelling geomorphic response to environmental change in an upland catchment.** Hydrological Processes. 14: 2031-2045.

Dudley, S.J.; Fischenich, J.C.; Abt, S.R. 1998. **Effects of woody debris entrapment on flow resistance.** Journal of the American Water Resources Association. 34: 1189-1197.

Faustini, J.M.; Jones, J.A. 2003. **Influence of large woody debris on channel morphology and dynamics in steep, boulder-rich mountain streams, western Cascades, Oregon.** Geomorphology. 51: 187-205.

Fitzpatrick, F.A.; Knox, J.C. 2004. **Spatial and temporal sensitivity of hydrogeomorphic response and recovery to deforestation, agriculture, and floods.** Physical Geography. 21: 89-108.

Gabbard, D.S.; Huang, C.; Norton, L.D.; Steinhardt, G.C. 1998. **Landscape position, surface hydraulic gradients and erosion processes.** Earth Surface Processes and Landforms. 23: 83-93.

Geyer, W.A.; Neppl, T.; Brooks, K.; Carlisle, J. 2000. **Woody vegetation protects streambank stability during the 1993 flood in central Kansas.** Journal of Soil and Water Conservation. 55: 483-486.

Gippel, C.J. 1995. **Environmental hydraulics of large woody debris.** Journal of Environmental Engineering. 121: 388-395.

Gomi, T.; Sidle, R.C.; Richardson, J.S. 2002. **Understanding processes and downstream linkages of headwater systems.** BioScience. 52: 905-916.

Hack, J.T.; Goodlett, J.C. 1960. **Geomorphology and forest ecology of a mountain region in the central Appalachians.** Prof. Pap. 347. Washington, DC: U.S. Government Printing Office. 66 p.

Hansen, W.F. 2001. **Identifying stream types and management implications.** Forest Ecology and Management. 143: 39-46.

Harmon, M.E.; Franklin, J.F.; Swanson, F.J.; Scollins, P.; Gregory, S.V.; Lattin, J.D.; Anderson, N.H.; Cline, S.P.; Aumen, N.G.; Sedell, J.R.; Lienkaemper, G.W.; Cromack, J.; Cummins, K.W. 1986. **Ecology of coarse woody debris in temperate ecosystems.** Advances in Ecological Research. 15: 133-302.

Harrelson, C.C.; Rawlins, C.L.; Potyondy, J.P. 1994. **Stream channel reference sites: an illustrated guide to field techniques.** Gen. Tech. Rep. RM-245. Fort Collins, CO: U.S. Department of Agriculture, Forest Service, Rocky Mountain Forest and Range Experiment Station. 61 p.

Hedman, C.M.; Van Lear, D.H.; Swank, W.T. 1996. **Instream large woody debris loading and riparian forest seral stage associations in the southern Appalachian Mountains.** Canadian Journal of Forest Research. 26: 1218-1227.

Heede, B.H. 1992. **Stream dynamics: an overview for land managers.** Gen. Tech. Rep. RM-72. Fort Collins, CO: U.S. Department of Agriculture, Forest Service, Rocky Mountain Forest and Range Experiment Station. 26 p.

Hicks, N.S.; Smith, J.A.; Miller, A.J.; Nelson, P.A. 2005. **Catastrophic flooding from an orographic thunderstorm in the central Appalachians.** Water Resources Research. 41: W12428. Abstract.

Holtan, H.N.; Creitz, N.R. 1969. **Influence of soils, vegetation, and geomorphology on elements of the flood hydrograph: floods and their computation.** Ceuterick, Belgium: UNESCO: 2: 755-767.

Jeffries, R.; Darby, S.E.; Sear, D.A. 2003. **The influence of vegetation and organic debris on flood-plain sediment dynamics: case study of a low-order stream in the New Forest, England.** Geomorphology. 51: 61-80.

Kirchner, J.W.; Finkel, R.C.; Riebe, C.S.; Granger, D.E.; Clayton, J.L.; King, J.G.; Megahan, W.F. 2001. **Mountain erosion over 10 yr, 10 k.y., and 10 m.y. time scales.** Geology. 29: 591-594.

Macklin, M.G.; Lewin, J. 2003. **River sediments, great floods and centennial-scale Holocene climate change.** Journal of Quaternary Science. 18: 101-105.

Maser, C.; Tarran, R.F.; Trappe, J.M.; Franklin, J.F. 1988. **From the forest to the sea: a story of fallen trees.** Gen. Tech. Rep. PNW-229. Portland, OR: U.S. Department of Agriculture, Forest Service, Pacific Northwest Forest and Range Experiment Station. 153 p.

Miller, A.J. 1990. **Flood hydrology and geomorphic effectiveness in the Central Appalachians.** Earth Surface Processes and Landforms. 15: 119-134.

Miller, D.J.; Benda, L.E. 2000. **Effects of punctuated sediment supply on valley floor landforms and sediment transport.** Geological Society of America Bulletin. 112: 1814-1824.

Myers, T.; Swanson, S. 1996. **Stream morphological impact of and recovery from major flooding in north-central Nevada.** Physical Geography. 17: 431-445.

Nakamura, F.; Swanson, F.J. 1993. **Effects of coarse woody debris on morphology and sediment storage of a mountain stream system in western Oregon.** Earth Surface Processes and Landforms. 18: 43-61.

Neary, D.G.; Swift, L.W. 1987. **Rainfall thresholds for triggering a debris avalanching event in the southern Appalachian Mountains.** In: Costa, J.E.; Wieczorek, G.F., eds. Reviews in engineering geology - debris flows/avalanches: process, recognition, and mitigation. Boulder, CO: Geological Society of America: 7: 81-92.

Neary, D.G.; Swift, L.W.; Manning, D.M.; Burns, R.G. 1986. **Debris avalanching in the southern Appalachians: an influence on forest soil formation.** Soil Science Society of America Journal. 50: 465-471.

Patten, D.T.; Stevens, L.E. 2001. **Restoration of the Colorado River ecosystem using planned flooding.** Ecological Applications. 11: 633-634.

Patten, D.T.; Harpman, D.A.; Voita, M.I.; Randle, T.J. 2001. **A managed flood on the Colorado River: background, objectives, design, and implementation.** Ecological Applications. 11: 635-643.

Paybins, K.S. 2003. **Flow origin, drainage area, and hydrologic characteristics of headwater streams in the mountaintop coal-mining region of southern West Virginia, 2001-01.** Water Resour. Invest. Rep. 02-4300. Charleston, WV: U.S. Geological Survey. 20 p.

Phillips, J.D. 2002. **Geomorphic impacts of flash flooding in a forested headwater basin.** Journal of Hydrology. 269: 236-250.

Robinson, J.S.; Sivapalan, M.; Snell, J.D. 1995. **On the relative roles of hillslope processes, channel routing, and network geomorphology in the hydrologic response of natural catchments.** Water Resources Research. 31: 3089-3101.

Robison, E.G.; Beschta, R.L. 1990. **Coarse woody debris and channel morphology interactions for undisturbed streams in southeast Alaska, U.S.A.** Earth Surface Processes and Landforms. 15: 149-156.

Rosgen, D.L. 1994. **A classification of natural rivers.** Catena. 22: 169-199.

Ruhlman, M.B.; Nutter, W.L. 1999. **Channel morphology evolution and overbank flow in the Georgia Piedmont.** Journal of the American Water Resources Division. 35: 277-290.

Shankman, D.; Samson, S.A. 1991. **Channelization effects on Obion River flooding, western Tennessee.** Water Resources Bulletin. 27: 247-254.

Sidle, R.C.; Onda, Y. 2004. **Hydrogeomorphology: an overview of an emerging science.** Hydrological Processes. 18: 597-602.

Sidle, R.C.; Tsuboyama, Y.; Noguchi, S.; Hosoda, I.; Fujieda, M.; Shimizu, T. 2000. **Stormflow generation in steep forested headwaters: a linked hydrogeomorphic paradigm.** Hydrological Processes. 14: 369-385.

Smith, R.D.; Sidle, R.C.; Porter, P.E.; Noel, J.R. 1993. **Effect of experimental removal of woody debris on the channel morphology of a forest, gravel-bed stream.** Journal of Hydrology. 152: 153-178.

Stover, S.C.; Montgomery, D.R. 2001. **Channel change and flooding, Skokomish River, Washington.** Journal of Hydrology. 243: 272-286.

Svec, J.R.; Kolka, R.K.; Stringer, J.W. 2005. **Defining perennial, intermittent, and ephemeral channels in eastern Kentucky: application to forestry best management practices.** Forest Ecology and Management. 214: 170-182.

Tsuboyama, Y.; Sidle, R.C.; Noguchi, S.; Murakami, S.; Shimizu, T. 2000. **A zero-order basin – its contribution to catchment hydrology and internal hydrological processes.** Hydrological Processes. 14: 387-401.

Wells, W.G. 1987. **The effects of fire on the generation of debris flows in southern California.** In: Costa, J.E.; Wieczorek, G.F., eds. Reviews in engineering geology - debris flows/avalanches: process, recognition, and mitigation. Boulder, CO: Geological Society of America: 7: 105-114.

White, E.L. 1975. **Factor analysis of drainage basin properties: classification of flood behavior in** terms of basin geomorphology. Water Resources Bulletin. 11: 676-687.

White, W.R.; Bettess, R.; Paris, E. 1982. **Analytical approach to river regime.** Journal of the Hydraulics Division-ASCE. 108: 1179-1193.

Wieczorek, G.F. 1987. **Effect of rainfall intensity and duration on debris flows in central Santa Cruz Mountains, California.** In: Costa, J.E.; Wieczorek, G.F., eds. Reviews in engineering geology - debris flows/avalanches: process, recognition, and mitigation. Boulder, CO: Geological Society of America: 7: 93-104.

Wolman, M.G.; Gerson, R. 1978. **Relative scales of time and effectiveness of climate in watershed geomorphology.** Earth Surface Processes and Landforms. 3: 189-208.

Wondzell, S.M.; Swanson, F.J. 1999. **Floods, channel change, and the hyporheic zone.** Water Resources Research. 35: 555-567.

Forest Operations and Management Effects

Beasley, R.S. 1979. **Intensive site preparation and sediment losses on steep watersheds in the Gulf Coastal Plain.** Soil Science Society of America Journal. 43: 412-417.

Beasley, R.S.; Granillo, A.B. 1986. **Sediment losses from forest management: mechanical vs. chemical site preparation after clearcutting.** Journal of Environmental Quality. 15: 413-416.

Beasley, R.S.; Granillo, A.B. 1988. **Sediment and water yields from managed forests on flat coastal plain sites.** Water Resources Bulletin. 24: 361-388.

Bent, G.C. 2001. **Effects of forest-management activities on runoff components and ground-water recharge to Quabbin Reservoir, central Massachusetts.** Forest Ecology and Management. 143: 115-129.

Beschta, R.L.; Pyles, M.R.; Skaugset, A.E.; Surfleet, C.G. 2000. **Peakflow responses to forest practices in the western cascades of Oregon, USA.** Journal of Hydrology. 233: 102-120.

Blackburn, W.H.; Wood, J.C.; DeHaven, M.G. 1986. **Storm flow and sediment losses from site-prepared forestland in East Texas.** Water Resources Research. 22: 776-784.

Bosch, J.M.; Hewlett, J.D. 1982. **A review of catchment experiments to determine the effect of vegetation changes on water yield and evapotranspiration.** Journal of Hydrology. 55: 3-23.

Bowling, L.C.; Lettenmaier, D.P. 2001. **The effects of forest roads and harvest on catchment hydrology in a mountainous maritime environment.** In: Wigmosta, M.S.; Burges, S.J., eds. Land use and watersheds: human influence on hydrology and geomorphology in urban and forest areas. Washington, DC: American Geophysical Union: 145-164.

Bowling, L.C.; Storck, P.; Lettenmaier, D.P. 2000. **Hydrologic effects of logging in western Washington, United States.** Water Resources Research. 36: 3223-3240.

Brooks, K.N.; Ffolliott, P.F.; Gregersen, H.M.; DeBano, L.F. 2003. **Hydrology and the management of watersheds.** 3d ed. Ames, IA: Iowa State Press. 574 p.

Buttle, J.M.; Metcalfe, R.A. 2000. **Boreal forest disturbance and streamflow response, northeastern Ontario.** Canadian Journal of Fisheries and Aquatic Sciences. 57: 5-18.

Buttle, J.M.; Hazlett, P.W.; Murray, C.D.; Creed, I.F.; Jeffries, D.S.; Semkin, R. 2001. **Prediction of groundwater characteristics in forested and harvested basins during spring snowmelt using a topographic index.** Hydrological Processes. 15: 3389-3407.

Caissie, D.; Jolicoeur, S.; Bouchard, M.; Poncet, E. 2002. **Comparison of streamflow between pre and post timber harvesting in Catamaran Brook (Canada).** Journal of Hydrology. 258: 232-248.

Cornish, P.M. 1993. **The effects of logging and forest regeneration on water yields in a moist eucalypt forest in New South Wales, Australia.** Journal of Hydrology. 150: 301-322.

Cornish, P.M.; Vertessy, R.A. 2001. **Forest age-induced changes in evapotranspiration and water yield in a eucalypt forest.** Journal of Hydrology. 242: 43-63.

Curry, R.A.; Scruton, D.A.; Clarke, K.D. 2002. **The thermal regimes of brook trout incubation habitats and evidence of changes during forestry operations.** Canadian Journal of Forest Research. 32: 1200-1207.

Dahlgren, R.A.; Driscoll, C.T. 1994. **The effects of whole-tree clear-cutting on soil processes at the Hubbard Brook Experimental Forest, New Hampshire, USA.** Plant and Soil. 158: 239-262.

Davies, P.E.; Nelson, M. 1993. **The effect of steep slope logging on fine sediment infiltration into the beds of ephemeral and perennial streams of the Dazzler Range, Tasmania, Australia.** Journal of Hydrology. 150: 481-504.

Dietterick, B.C.; Lynch, J.A. 1989. **Cumulative hydrologic effects on stormflows of successive clearcuts on a small headwater basin.** In: Proceedings of the symposium on headwaters hydrology; [When and Where held unknown]. Bethesda, MD: American Water Resources Association: 473-485.

Douglass, J.E. 1983. **The potential for water yield augmentation from forest management in the eastern United States.** Water Resources Bulletin. 19: 351-358.

Douglass, J.E.; Swank, W.T. 1972. **Streamflow modification through management of eastern forests.** Res. Pap. SE-94. Asheville, NC: U.S. Department of Agriculture, Forest Service, Southeastern Forest Experiment Station. 15 p.

Dykes, A.P.; Thornes, J.B. 2000. **Hillslope hydrology in tropical rainforest steeplands in Brunei.** Hydrological Processes. 14: 215-235.

Edwards, P.; Kochenderfer, J.N. 1991. **Effects of forest fertilization on stream water chemistry in the Appalachians.** Water Resources Bulletin. 27: 265-274.

Fitzpatrick, F.A.; Knox, J.C. 2004. **Spatial and temporal sensitivity of hydrogeomorphic response and recovery to deforestation, agriculture, and floods.** Physical Geography. 21: 89-108.

Gottfried, G.J. 1991. **Moderate timber harvesting increases water yields from an Arizona mixed conifer watershed.** Water Resources Research. 27: 537-547.

Grayson, R.B.; Haydon, S.R.; Jayasuriya, M.D.A.; Finlayson, B.L. 1993. **Water quality in mountain ash forests - separating the impacts of roads from those of logging operations.** Journal of Hydrology. 150: 459-480.

Guillemette, F.; Plamondon, A.P.; Prevost, M.; Levesque, D. 2005. **Rainfall generated stormflow response to clearcutting a boreal forest: peak flow comparison with 50 world-wide basin studies.** Journal of Hydrology. 302: 137-153.

Hansen, W.F. 2001. **Identifying stream types and management implications.** Forest Ecology and Management. 143: 39-46.

Harr, R.D. 1983. **Potential for augmenting water yield through forest practices in western Washington and western Oregon.** Water Resources Bulletin. 19: 383-393.

Harr, R.D.; Harper, W.C.; Krygier, J.T.; Hsieh, F.S. 1975. **Changes in storm hydrographs after road building and clear-cutting on the Oregon Coast Range.** Water Resources Research. 11: 436-444.

Hatchel, G.E.; Ralston, C.W.; Foil, R.R. 1970. **Soil disturbances in logging.** Journal of Forestry. 68: 772-775.

Hewlett, J.D.; Helvey, J.D. 1970. **Effects of forest clear-felling on the storm hydrograph.** Water Resources Research. 6: 768-782.

Hibbert, A.D. 1983. **Water yield improvement potential by vegetation management on western rangelands.** Water Resources Bulletin. 19: 375-381.

Hornbeck, J.W. 1973. **Stormwater flow from hardwood forested and cleared watersheds in New Hampshire.** Water Resources Research. 9: 346-354.

Hornbeck, J.W.; Pierce, R.S.; Federer, C.A. 1970. **Streamflow changes after forest clearing in New England.** Water Resources Research. 6: 1124-1132.

Hornbeck, J.W.; Martin, C.W.; Eagar, C. 1997. **Summary of water yield experiments at Hubbard Brook Experimental Forest.** Canadian Journal of Forest Research. 27: 2043-2052.

Hornbeck, J.W.; Adams, M.B.; Corbett, E.S.; Verry, E.S.; Lynch, J.A. 1993. **Long-term impacts of forest treatments on water yields: a summary for northeastern USA.** Journal of Hydrology. 150: 323-344.

Hornbeck, J.W.; Adams, M.B.; Corbett, E.S.; Verry, E.S.; Lynch, J.A. 1995. **A summary of water yield experiments on hardwood forested watersheds in northeastern U.S.** In: Gottschalk, K.W.; Fosbroke, S.L.C., eds. Proceedings of 10th central hardwoods forest conference; 1995 March 5-8; Morgantown, WV. Gen. Tech. Rep. NE-197. Radnor, PA: U.S. Department of Agriculture, Forest Service, Northeastern Forest Experiment Station: 282-295.

Hornbeck, J.W.; Martin, C.W.; Pierce, R.S.; Bormann, H.; Likens, G.E.; Easton, J.S. 1987. **Clearcutting northern hardwoods: effects on hydrologic and nutrient ion budgets.** Forest Science. 32: 667-686.

Hursh, C.R. 1951. **Watershed aspects of the New York water supply problems.** Journal of Forestry. 49: 442-444.

Jackson, C.R.; Martin, J.K.; Leigh, D.S.; West, L.T. 2005. **A southeastern piedmont watershed sediment budget: evidence for a multi-millennial agricultural legacy.** Journal of Soil and Water Conservation. 60: 298-310.

Jayasuriya, M.D.A.; Dunn, G.; Benyon, R.; O'Shaughnessy, P.J. 1993. **Some factors affecting water yield from mountain ash (*Eucalyptus regnans*) dominated forests in southeast Australia.** Journal of Hydrology. 150: 345-367.

Johnson, R. 1998. **The forest cycle and low river flows: a review of UK and international studies.** Forest Ecology and Management. 109: 1-7.

Jones, J.A. 2000. **Hydrologic processes and peak discharge response to forest removal, regrowth, and roads in 10 small experimental basins, western Cascades, Oregon.** Water Resources Research. 36: 2621-2642.

Jones, J.A.; Grant, G.E. 1996. **Peak flow responses to clear-cutting and roads in small and large basins, western Cascades, Oregon.** Water Resources Research. 32: 959-974.

Jones, J.A.; Post, D.A. 2004. **Seasonal and successional streamflow response to forest cutting and regrowth in the northwest and eastern United States.** Water Resources Research. 40: 1-19.

Kattelmann, R.C.; Berg, N.H.; Rector, J. 1983. **The potential for increasing streamflow from Sierra Nevada watersheds.** Water Resources Bulletin. 19: 395-402.

Keller, H.M. 1988. **European experiences in long-term forest hydrology research.** In: Swank, W.T.; Crossley, D.A., Jr., eds. Forest hydrology and ecology at Coweeta. New York: Springer-Verlag: 407-414.

Kochenderfer, J.N.; Wendel, G.W. 1983. **Plant succession and hydrologic recovery on a deforested and herbicided watershed.** Forest Science. 29: 545-558.

Kochenderfer, J.N.; Edwards, P.; Helvey, J.D. 1990. **Land management and water yield in the Appalachians.** In: Watershed planning and analysis in action symposium proceedings; 1990 July 9-11; Durango, CO. New York: American Society of Civil Engineers: 523-532.

Krutilla, J.V.; Bowes, M.D.; Sherman, P. 1983. Watershed management for joint production of water and timber: a provisional assessment. Water Resources Bulletin. 19: 403-414.

LaMarche, J.L.; Lettenmaier, D.P. 2001. Effects of forest roads on flood flows in the Deschutes River, Washington. Earth Surface Processes and Landforms. 26: 115-134.

Lewis, J.; Mori, S.R.; Keppeler, E.T.; Ziemer, R.R. 2001. Impacts of logging on storm peak flows, flow volumes, and suspended sediment loads in Caspar Creek, California. In: Wigmosta, M.S.; Burges, S.J., eds. Land use and watersheds: human influence on hydrology and geomorphology in urban and forest areas. Washington, DC: American Geophysical Union: 85-125.

Lockaby, B.G.; Stanturf, J.A.; Messina, M.G. 1997. Effects of silvicultural activity on ecological processes in floodplain forests of the southern United States: a review of existing reports. Forest Ecology and Management. 90: 93-100.

Lockaby, B.G.; Clawson, R.G.; Flynn, K.; Rummer, R.; Meadows, S.; Stokes, B.; Stanturf, J. 1997. Influence of harvesting on biogeochemical exchange in sheetflow and soil processes in a eutrophic floodplain forest. Forest Ecology and Management. 90: 187-194.

Lu, S.-Y.; Cheng, J.D.; Brooks, K.N. 2001. Managing forests for watershed protection in Taiwan. Forest Ecology and Management. 143: 77-85.

Lull, H.W.; Reinhart, K.G. 1972. Forests and floods. Res. Pap. NE-226. Upper Darby, PA: U.S. Department of Agriculture, Forest Service, Northeastern Forest Experiment Station. 94 p.

Martin, C.W.; Hornbeck, J.W.; Likens, G.E.; Buso, D.C. 2000. Impacts of intensive harvesting on hydrology and nutrient dynamics of northern hardwood forests. Canadian Journal of Fisheries and Aquatic Sciences. 57: 19-29.

McDonald, B.R.; Trianosky, P. 1995. Assessment of, and management recommendations for, the plant communities and rare species of Camp Brookside, New River Gorge National River. Tech. Rep. 95-5. Elkins, WV: West Virginia Natural Heritage Program. 24 p.

Megahan, W.F. 1972. Logging, erosion, sedimentation: Are they dirty words? Journal of Forestry. 70: 403-407.

Megahan, W.F.; King, J.G.; Seyedbagheri, K.A. 1995. Hydrologic and erosional responses of a granitic watershed to helicopter logging and broadcast burning. Forest Science. 41: 777-795.

Meng, F.; Bourque, C.; Jewett, K.; Daugharty, D.; Arp, P. 1995. The Nashwaak Experimental Watershed Project: analysing effects of clearcutting on soil temperature, soil moisture, snowpack, snowmelt, and stream flow. Water, Air, and Soil Pollution. 82: 363-374.

Miller, E.L. 1984. Sediment yield and storm flow response to clear-cut harvest and site preparations in the Ouachita Mountains. Water Resources Research. 20: 471-475.

Miller, E.L.; Beasley, R.S.; Lawson, E.R. 1988. Forest harvest and site preparation effects on erosion and sedimentation in the Ouachita Mountains. Journal of Environmental Quality. 17: 219-225.

Neary, D.G.; Ffolliott, P.F.; Landsberg, J.D. 2005. Fire and streamflow regimes. In: Neary, D.G.; et al., eds. Wildland fire in ecosystem effects of fire on soils and water. Gen. Tech. Rep. RMRS-GTR-42. Ogden, UT: U.S. Department of Agriculture, Forest Service, Rocky Mountain Research Station: 4: 107-118.

Patric, J.H. 1973. Deforestation effects on soil moisture, streamflow, and water balance in the Central Appalachians. Res. Pap. NE-259. Upper Darby, PA: U.S. Department of Agriculture, Forest Service, Northeastern Forest Experiment Station. 12 p.

Patric, J.H. 1980. Effects of wood products harvest on forest soil and water relations. Journal of Environmental Quality. 9: 73-80.

Patric, J.H.; Reinhart, K.G. 1971. Hydrologic effects of deforesting two mountain watersheds in West Virginia. Water Resources Research. 7: 1182-1188.

Patric, J.H.; Evans, J.O.; Helvey, J.D. 1984. **Summary of sediment yield data from forested land use in the United States.** Journal of Forestry. 82: 101-104.

Perry, C.A.; Aldridge, B.N.; Ross, H.C. 2001. **Summary of significant floods in the United States, Puerto Rico, and the Virgin Islands, 1970 through 1989.** Water-Supply Pap. 2502. U.S. Geological Survey. http://ks.water.usgs.gov/Kansas/pubs/reports/wsp.2502.html (15 September 2005).

Pierce, R.S.; Hornbeck, J.W.; Martin, C.W.; Tritton, L.M.; Smith, C.T.; Federer, C.A.; Yawney, H.W. 1993. **Whole tree clearcutting in New England: manager's guide to impacts on soils, streams, and regeneration.** Gen. Tech. Rep. NE-172. Radnor, PA: U.S. Department of Agriculture, Forest Service, Northeastern Forest Experiment Station. 23 p.

Ponce, S.L.; Meiman, J.R. 1983. **Water yield augmentation through forest and range management - issues for the future.** Water Resources Bulletin. 19: 415-419.

Pothier, D.; Prevost, M.; Auger, I. 2003. **Using the shelterwood method to mitigate water table rise after forest harvesting.** Forest Ecology and Management. 179: 573-583.

Reinhart, K.G.; Eschner, A.R.; Trimble, G.R.J. 1963. **Effect on streamflow of four forest practices.** Res. Pap. NE-1. Upper Darby, PA: U.S. Department of Agriculture, Forest Service, Northeastern Forest Experiment Station. 79 p.

Robinson, M. 1986. **Changes in catchment runoff following drainage and afforestation.** Journal of Hydrology. 86: 71-84.

Robinson, M.; Dupeyrat, A. 2005. **Effects of commercial timber harvesting on streamflow regimes in the Plynlimon catchments, mid-Wales.** Hydrological Processes. 19: 1213-1226.

Robinson, M.; Cognard-Plancq, A.-L.; Cosandey, C.; David, J.; Durand, P.; Fuhrer, H.-W.; Hall, R.; Hendriques, M.O.; Marc, V.; McCarthy, R.; McDonnell, M.; Martin, C.W.; Nisbet, T.; O'Dea, P.; Rogers, M.; Zollner, A. 2003. **Studies on the impact of forests on peak flows and baseflows: a European perspective.** Forest Ecology and Management. 186: 85-97.

Rothacher, J. 1970. **Increases in water yield following clear-cut logging in the Pacific Northwest.** Water Resources Research. 6: 653-658.

Rowe, L.K.; Pearce, A.J. 1994. **Hydrology and related changes after harvesting native forest catchments and establishing *Pinus radiata* plantations. Part 2: The native forest water balance and changes in streamflow after harvesting.** Hydrological Processes. 8: 281-297.

Rowe, L.K.; Taylor, C.H. 1994. **Hydrology and related changes after harvesting native forest catchments and establishing *Pinus radiata* plantations. Part 3: Stream temperatures.** Hydrological Processes. 8: 299-310.

Rowe, L.K.; Pearce, A.J.; O'Loughlin, C.L. 1994. **Hydrology and related changes after harvesting native forest catchments and establishing *Pinus radiata* plantations. Part 1: Introduction to study.** Hydrological Processes. 8: 263-279.

Ruprecht, J.K.; Stoneman, G.L. 1993. **Water yield issues in the jarrah forest of southwestern Australia.** Journal of Hydrology. 150: 369-391.

Schmitz, M.F.; Atauri, J.A.; de Pablo, C.L.; de Agar, P.M.; Rescia, A.J.; Pineda, F.D. 1998. **Changes in land use in northern Spain: effects of forestry management on soil conservation.** Forest Ecology and Management. 109: 137-150.

Scott, D.F. 1993. **The hydrological effects of fire in South African mountain catchments.** Journal of Hydrology. 150: 409-432.

Sidle, R.C.; Tani, M.; Ziegler, A.D. 2006. **Catchment processes in Southeast Asia: atmospheric hydrologic, erosion, nutrient cycling, and management effects.** Forest Ecology and Management. 224: 1-4.

Smith, D.W.; Prepas, E.E.; Putz, G.; Burke, J.M.; Meyer, J.L.; Whitson, I. 2003. **The Forest Watershed and**

Riparian Disturbance Study: a multi-discipline initiative to evaluate and manage watershed disturbance on the Boreal Plain of Canada. Journal of Environmental Engineering and Science. 2: S1-S13.

Stednick, J.D. 1996. **Monitoring the effects of timber harvest on annual water yield.** Journal of Hydrology. 176: 79-95.

Stoneman, G.L. 1993. **Hydrological response to thinning a small jarrah (*Eucalyptus marginata*) forest catchment.** Journal of Hydrology. 150: 393-407.

Storck, P.; Bowling, L.C.; Wetherbee, P.; Lettenmaier, D.P. 1998. **Application of a GIS-based distributed hydrology model for prediction of forest harvest effects on peak stream flow in the Pacific Northwest.** Hydrological Processes. 12: 889-904.

Swank, W.T.; Swift, L.W.; Douglass, J.E. 1988. **Streamflow changes associated with forest cutting, species conversions, and natural disturbances.** In: Swank, W.T.; Crossley, D.A., Jr., eds. Forest hydrology and ecology at Coweeta. New York: Springer-Verlag: 297-312.

Swank, W.T.; Vose, J.M.; Elliott, K.J. 2001. **Long-term hydrologic and water quality responses following commercial clearcutting of mixed hardwoods on a southern Appalachian catchment.** Forest Ecology and Management. 143: 163-178.

Swanson, R.H. 1998. **Forest hydrology issues for the 21st century: a consultant's viewpoint.** Journal of the American Water Resources Division. 34: 755-763.

Tague, C.; Band, L.E. 2001. **Simulating the impact of road construction and forest harvesting on hydrologic response.** Earth Surface Processes and Landforms. 26: 135-151.

Thomas, R.B.; Megahan, W.F. 1998. **Peak flow responses to clear-cutting and roads in small and large basins, western Cascades, Oregon: a second opinion.** Water Resources Research. 34: 3393-3403.

Thornton, K.W.; Holbrook, S.P.; Stolte, K.L.; Landy, R.B. 2000. **Effects of forest management practices on Mid-Atlantic streams.** Environmental Monitoring and Assessment. 63: 31-41.

Troendle, C.A. 1983. **The potential for water yield augmentation from forest management in the Rocky Mountain Region.** Water Resources Bulletin. 19: 359-373.

Troendle, C.A.; King, R.M. 1985. **The effect of timber harvest on the Fool Creek Watershed, 30 years later.** Water Resources Research. 21: 1915-1922.

Troendle, C.A.; Wilcox, M.S.; Bevenger, G.S.; Porth, L.S. 2001. **The Coon Creek Water Yield Augmentation Project: implementation of timber harvesting technology to increase streamflow.** Forest Ecology and Management. 143: 179-187.

Twery, M.J.; Hornbeck, J.W. 2001. **Incorporating water goals into forest management at a local level.** Forest Ecology and Management. 143: 87-93.

Ursic, S.J. 1991. **Hydrologic effects of clearcutting and stripcutting loblolly pine in the coastal plain.** Water Resources Bulletin. 27: 925-937.

Yeakley, J.A.; Coleman, D.C.; Haines, B.L.; Kloeppel, B.D.; Meyer, J.L.; Swank, W.T.; Argo, B.W.; Deal, J.M.; Taylor, S.F. 2003. **Hillslope nutrient dynamics following upland riparian vegetation disturbance.** Ecosystems. 6: 154-167.

Nonforest Land Use Effects

Ataroff, M.; Rada, F. 2000. **Deforestation impact on water dynamics in a Venezuelan Andean cloud forest.** Ambio. 29: 440-444.

Bonta, J.V.; Amerman, C.R.; Harlukowicz, T.J.; Dick, W.A. 1997. **Impact of coal surface mining on three Ohio watersheds - surface water hydrology.** Journal of the American Water Resources Division. 33: 907-917.

Bruins, R.J.F.; Shuming, C.; Shijian, C.; Mitsch, W.J. 1998. **Ecological engineering strategies to reduce flooding damage to wetland crops in central China.** Ecological Engineering. 11: 231-259.

Brzozowski, C. 2004. **A flood of concern in Roanoke.** American Forests. 110: 38-43.

Calder, I.R. 1993. **Hydrologic effects of land-use change.** In: Maidment, D.R., ed. Handbook of hydrology. New York: McGraw-Hill: 13.1-13.50.

Carlson, T.N.; Arthur, S.T. 2000. **The impact of land use - land cover changes due to urbanization on surface microclimate and hydrology: a satellite perspective.** Global and Planetary Change. 25: 49-65.

Check, L.M. 1997. **Drainage planning and control in the urban environment: the Singapore experience.** Environmental Monitoring and Assessment. 44: 183-197.

Clark, J.J.; Wilcock, P.R. 2000. **Effects of land-use change on channel morphology in northeastern Puerto Rico.** Geological Society of America Bulletin. 112: 1763-1777.

Criss, R.E.; Shock, E.L. 2001. **Flood enhancement through flood control.** Geology. 29: 875-878.

Curtis, W.R. 1969. **Effects of strip mining on the hydrology of small mountain watersheds in Appalachia.** In: Hutnick, R.J.; Davis, G., eds. Ecology and reclamation of devastated land. New York: Gordon and Breach: 145-157.

Curtis, W.R. 1979. **Surface mining and the hydrologic balance.** Mining Congress Journal. 65: 35-40.

DeWalle, D.R.; Swistock, B.R.; Johnson, T.E.; McGuire, K.J. 2000. **Potential effects of climate change and urbanization on mean annual streamflow in the United States.** Water Resources Research. 36: 2655-2664.

Dunn, S.M.; Mackay, R. 1995. **Spatial variation in evapotranspiration and the influence of land use on catchment hydrology.** Journal of Hydrology. 171: 49-73.

Fitzpatrick, F.A.; Knox, J.C. 2004. **Spatial and temporal sensitivity of hydrogeomorphic response and recovery to deforestation, agriculture, and floods.** Physical Geography. 21: 89-108.

Gardi, C. 2001. **Land use, agronomic management and water quality in a small northern Italian watershed.** Agricultural Ecosystems and Environment. 87: 1-12.

Gaume, E.; Livet, M.; Desbordes, M. 2003. **Study of the hydrological processes during the Avene River extraordinary flood (south of France), 6-7 October 1997.** Physics and Chemistry of the Earth. 28: 263-267.

Gaume, E.; Livet, M.; Desbordes, M.; Villeneuve, J.-P. 2004. **Hydrological analysis of the River Aude, France, flash flood on 12 and 13 November 1999.** Journal of Hydrology. 286: 135-154.

Guebert, M.D.; Gardner, T.W. 2001. **Macropore flow on a reclaimed surface mine: infiltration and hillslope hydrology.** Geomorphology. 39: 151-169.

Guild, L.S.; Cohen, W.B.; Kauffman, J.B. 2004. **Detection of deforestation and land conversion in Rondonia, Brazil using change detection techniques.** International Journal of Remote Sensing. 25: 731-750.

Hollis, G.E. 1975. **The effect of urbanization on floods of different recurrence intervals.** Water Resources Research. 11: 431-435.

Holman, I.P.; Hollis, J.M.; Bramley, M.E.; Thompson, T.R.E. 2003. **The contribution of soil structural degradation to catchment flooding: a preliminary investigation of the 2000 floods in England and Wales.** Hydrology and Earth System Sciences. 7: 754-765.

Hutnik, R.J.; Davis, G., eds. 1973a. **Ecology and reclamation of devastated land.** New York: Gordon and Breach. 538 p. Vol. 1.

Hutnik, R.J.; Davis, G., eds. 1973b. **Ecology and reclamation of devastated land.** New York: Gordon and Breach. 504 p. Vol. 2.

Jackson, C.R.; Martin, J.K.; Leigh, D.S.; West, L.T. 2005. **A southeastern piedmont watershed sediment budget: evidence for a multi-millennial agricultural legacy.** Journal of Soil and Water Conservation. 60: 298-310.

Kim, Y.; Engel, B.A.; Lim, K.J.; Larson, V.; Duncan, B. 2002. **Runoff impacts of land-use change in Indian River Lagoon watershed.** Journal of Hydrologic Engineering. 7: 245-251.

Kirkby, M.J.; Bracken, L.; Reaney, S. 2002. **The influence of land use, soils and topography on the delivery of hillslope runoff to channels in SE Spain.** Earth Surface Processes and Landforms. 27: 1459-1473.

Klijn, F.; van Buuren, M.; van Rooij, S. 2004. **Flood-risk management strategies for an uncertain future: living with Rhine river floods in the Netherlands.** Ambio. 33: 141-147.

Klocking, B.; Haberlandt, U. 2002. **Impact of land use changes on water dynamics - a case study in temperate meso and macroscale river basins.** Physics and Chemistry of the Earth. 27: 619-629.

Knox, J.C. 2001. **Agricultural influence on landscape sensitivity in the Upper Mississippi River Valley.** Catena. 42: 193-224.

Lal, R. 1997. **Deforestation effects on soil degradation and rehabilitation in western Nigeria. IV. Hydrology and water quality.** Land Degradation and Development. 8: 95-126.

Lewis, D.C. 1968. **Annual hydrologic response to watershed conversion from oak woodland to annual grassland.** Water Resources Research. 4: 59-72.

Longfield, S.A.; Macklin, M.G. 1999. **The influence of recent environmental change on flooding and sediment fluxes in the Yorkshire Ouse basin.** Hydrological Processes. 13: 1051-1066.

Lull, H.W.; Reinhart, K.G. 1972. **Forests and floods.** Res. Pap. NE-226. Upper Darby, PA: U.S. Department of Agriculture, Forest Service, Northeastern Forest Experiment Station. 94 p.

Miller, M.W.; Nudds, T.D. 1996. **Prairie landscape change and flooding in the Mississippi River Valley.** Conservation Biology. 10: 847-853.

Nelson, E.J.; Booth, D.B. 2002. **Sediment sources in an urbanizing, mixed land-use watershed.** Journal of Hydrology. 264: 51-68.

Phillips, J.D. 2004. **Impacts of surface mine valley fills on headwater floods in eastern Kentucky.** Environmental Geology. 45: 367-380.

Robinson, M.; Gannon, B.; Schuch, M. 1991. **A comparison of the hydrology of moorland under natural conditions, agricultural use, and forestry.** Hydrological Sciences Journal. 36: 565-577.

Stover, S.C.; Montgomery, D.R. 2001. **Channel change and flooding, Skokomish River, Washington.** Journal of Hydrology. 243: 272-286.

Striffler, W.D. 1973. **Surface mining disturbance and water quality in eastern Kentucky.** In: Hutnick, R.J.; Davis, G., eds. Ecology and reclamation of devastated land. New York: Gordon and Breach: 1: 175-191.

Vesterby, M.; Krupa, K.S. 1997. **Major uses of land in the United States, 1997.** Stat. Bull. 973. Washington, DC: U.S. Department of Agriculture, Economic Research Service. 60 p.

Wahl, N.A.; Bens, O.; Schafer, B.; Huttl, R.F. 2003. **Impact of changes in land use management on soil hydrologic properties: hydraulic conductivity, water repellency, and water retention.** Physics and Chemistry of the Earth. 28: 1377-1387.

Ziegler, A.D.; Giambelluca, T.W.; Sutherland, R.A.; Nullet, M.A.; Yarnasarn, S.; Pinthong, J.; Preechapanya, P.; Jaiaee, S. 2004. **Toward understanding the cumulative impacts of roads in upland agricultural watersheds of northern Thailand.** Agricultural Ecosystems and Environment. 104: 145-158.

Soil Disturbance, Roads, and Best Management Practices

Arthur, M.A.; Coltharp, G.B.; Brown, D.L. 1998. **Effects of best management practices on forest streamwater quality in eastern Kentucky.** Journal of the American Water Resources Division. 34: 481-495.

Aust, W.M.; Blinn, C. 2004. **Forestry best management practices for timber harvesting and site preparation in the eastern United States - an overview of water quality and productivity research during the past 20 years.** Water, Air, and Soil Pollution: Focus. 4: 5-36.

Beasley, R.S. 1979. **Intensive site preparation and sediment losses on steep watersheds in the Gulf Coastal Plain.** Soil Science Society of America Journal. 43: 412-417.

Blackburn, W.H.; Wood, J.C.; DeHaven, M.G. 1986. **Storm flow and sediment losses from site-prepared forestland in East Texas.** Water Resources Research. 22: 776-784.

Bowling, L.C.; Lettenmaier, D.P. 2001. **The effects of forest roads and harvest on catchment hydrology in a mountainous maritime environment.** In: Wigmosta, M.S.; Burges, S.J., eds. Land use and watersheds: human influence on hydrology and geomorphology in urban and forest areas. Washington, DC: American Geophysical Union: 145-164.

Bowling, L.C.; Storck, P.; Lettenmaier, D.P. 2000. **Hydrologic effects of logging in western Washington, United States.** Water Resources Research. 36: 3223-3240.

Bren, L.J. 1993. **Riparian zone, stream, and floodplain issues: a review.** Journal of Hydrology. 150: 277-299.

Brooks, A.P.; Gehrke, P.C.; Jansen, J.D.; Abbe, T.B. 2004. **Experimental reintroduction of woody debris on the Williams River, NSW: geomorphic and ecological responses.** River Research and Applications. 20: 513-536.

Clark, G.M. 1987. **Debris slide and debris flow historical events in the Appalachians south of the glacial border.** In: Costa, J.E.; Wieczorek, G.F., eds. Reviews in engineering geology - debris flows/avalanches: process, recognition, and mitigation. Boulder, CO: Geological Society of America: 7: 125-138.

Croke, J.; Hairsine, P.; Fogarty, P. 2001. **Soil recovery from track construction and harvesting changes in surface infiltration, erosion, and delivery rates with time.** Forest Ecology and Management. 143: 3-12.

Croke, J.; Mockler, S.; Hairsine, P.; Fogarty, P. 2006. **Relative contributions of runoff and sediment from sources within a road prism and implications for total sediment delivery.** Earth Surface Processes and Landforms. 31: 457-468.

Davies, P.E.; Nelson, M. 1993. **The effect of steep slope logging on fine sediment infiltration into the beds of ephemeral and perennial streams of the Dazzler Range, Tasmania, Australia.** Journal of Hydrology. 150: 481-504.

Dunne, T. 1998. **Critical data requirements for prediction of erosion and sedimentation in mountain drainage basins.** Journal of the American Water Resources Association. 34: 795-808.

Egan, E.F. 1999. **Do foresters and logging contracts matter?** Journal of Forestry. 97: 36-39.

Elliott, W.J.; Foltz, R.B.; Luce, C.H. 1999. **Modelling low-volume road erosion.** In: Proceedings of the 7th international conference on low-volume roads; 1999 May 23-26; Baton Rouge, LA. Washington, DC: National Academy Press: 2: 244-247.

Geyer, W.A.; Neppl, T.; Brooks, K.; Carlisle, J. 2000. **Woody vegetation protects streambank stability during the 1993 flood in central Kansas.** Journal of Soil and Water Conservation. 55: 483-486.

Gippel, C.J. 1995. **Environmental hydraulics of large woody debris.** Journal of Environmental Engineering. 121: 388-395.

Gomi, T.; Sidle, R.C.; Noguchi, S.; Negishi, J.N.; Nik, A.R.; Sasaki, S. 2006. **Sediment and wood accumulations in humid tropical headwater streams: effects of logging and riparian buffers.** Forest Ecology and Management. 224: 166-175.

Grayson, R.B.; Haydon, S.R.; Jayasuriya, M.D.A.; Finlayson, B.L. 1993. **Water quality in mountain** ash forests - separating the impacts of roads from those of logging operations. Journal of Hydrology. 150: 459-480.

Greacen, E.L.; Sands, R. 1980. **Compaction of forest soils - a review.** Australian Journal of Forest Research. 18: 163-189.

Gucinski, H.; Furniss, M.J.; Ziemer, R.R.; Brookes, M.H., eds. 2001. **Forest roads: a synthesis of scientific information.** Gen. Tech. Rep. PNW-509. Portland, OR: U.S. Department of Agriculture, Forest Service, Pacific Northwest Research Station. 103 p.

Haehnel, R.B.; Daly, S.F. 2004. **Maximum impact force of woody debris on floodplain structures.** Journal of Hydrologic Engineering. 130: 112-120.

Harr, R.D.; Harper, W.C.; Krygier, J.T.; Hsieh, F.S. 1975. **Changes in storm hydrographs after road building and clear-cutting on the Oregon Coast Range.** Water Resources Research. 11: 436-444.

Hatchel, G.E.; Ralston, C.W.; Foil, R.R. 1970. **Soil disturbances in logging.** Journal of Forestry. 68: 772-775.

Haupt, H.F. 1959. **Road and slope characteristics affecting sediment movement from logging roads.** Journal of Forestry. 57: 329-332.

Helvey, J.D.; Kochenderfer, J.N. 1988. **Culvert sizes needed for small drainage areas in the central Appalachians.** Northern Journal of Applied Forestry. 5: 123-127.

Holman, I.P.; Hollis, J.M.; Bramley, M.E.; Thompson, T.R.E. 2003. **The contribution of soil structural degradation to catchment flooding: a preliminary investigation of the 2000 floods in England and Wales.** Hydrology and Earth System Sciences. 7: 754-765.

Hood, S.M.; Zedaker, S.M.; Aust, W.M.; Smith, D.W. 2002. **Universal Soil Loss Equation (USLE) predicted soil loss for harvesting regimes in Appalachian hardwoods.** Northern Journal of Applied Forestry. 19: 53-58.

Jackson, C.R.; Martin, J.K.; Leigh, D.S.; West, L.T. 2005. **A southeastern piedmont watershed sediment budget: evidence for a multi-millennial agricultural legacy.** Journal of Soil and Water Conservation. 60: 298-310.

Jones, J.A.; Grant, G.E. 1996. **Peak flow responses to clear-cutting and roads in small and large basins, western Cascades, Oregon.** Water Resources Research. 32: 959-974.

Jones, J.A.; Swanson, F.J.; Wemple, B.C.; Snyder, K.U. 2000. **Effects of roads on hydrology, geomorphology, and disturbance patches in stream networks.** Conservation Biology. 14: 76-85.

Keim, R.F.; Skaugset, A.E. 2003. **Modelling effects of forest canopies on slope stability.** Hydrological Processes. 17: 1457-1467.

Keller, G.; Sherar, J. 2003. **Low-volume roads engineering - best management practices field guide.** Washington, DC: U.S. Department of Agriculture, Forest Service. 158 p. [Available on line: http://zietlow.com/manual/gk1/web.doc].

Kochenderfer, J.N. 1977. **Area in skidroads, truck roads, and landings in the central Appalachians.** Journal of Forestry. 8: 507-509.

Kochenderfer, J.N.; Helvey, J.D. 1987. **Using gravel to reduce soil losses from minimum-standard forest roads.** Journal of Soil and Water Conservation. 42: 46-50.

Kochenderfer, J.N.; Edwards, P.; Wood, E.F. 1997. **Hydrologic impacts of logging an Appalachian watershed using West Virginia's best management practices.** Northern Journal of Applied Forestry. 14: 207-218.

Lacey, S.T. 2000. **Runoff and sediment attenuation by undisturbed and lightly disturbed forest buffers.** Water, Air, and Soil Pollution. 122: 121-138.

LaMarche, J.L.; Lettenmaier, D.P. 2001. **Effects of forest roads on flood flows in the Deschutes River, Washington.** Earth Surface Processes and Landforms. 26: 115-134.

Lewis, J.; Mori, S.R.; Keppeler, E.T.; Ziemer, R.R. 2001. **Impacts of logging on storm peak flows, flow volumes, and suspended sediment loads in Caspar Creek, California.** In: Wigmosta, M.S.; Burges, S.J., eds. Land use and watersheds: human influence on hydrology and geomorphology in urban and forest areas. Washington, DC: American Geophysical Union: 85-125.

Luce, C.H.; Black, T.A. 2001. **Spatial and temporal patterns in erosion from forest roads.** In: Wigmosta, M.S.; Burges, S.J., eds. Land use and watersheds: human influence on hydrology and geomorphology in urban and forest areas. Washington, DC: American Geophysical Union: 165-178.

Lynch, J.A.; Corbett, E.S. 1990. **Evaluation of best management practices for controlling nonpoint source pollution from silvicultural operations.** Water Resources Bulletin. 26: 41-52.

Martin, C.W.; Hornbeck, J.W. 1994. **Logging in New England need not cause sedimentation of streams.** Northern Journal of Applied Forestry. 11: 17-23.

Martin, C.W.; Pierce, R.S. 1980. **Clearcutting patterns affect nitrate and calcium in streams of New Hampshire.** Journal of Forestry. 78: 268-276.

McClelland, D.E.; Foltz, R.B.; Falter, C.M.; Wilson, W.D.; Cundy, T.; Schuster, R.L.; Saubier, J.; Rabe, C.; Heinemann, R. 1999. **Relative effects on a low-volume road system of landslides resulting from episodic storms in northern Idaho.** In: Proceedings of the 7th international conference on low-volume roads; 1999 May 23-26; Baton Rouge, LA. Washington, DC: National Academy Press: 2: 235-243.

Megahan, W.F. 1972. **Logging, erosion, sedimentation: Are they dirty words?** Journal of Forestry. 70: 403-407.

Megahan, W.F.; King, J.G.; Seyedbagheri, K.A. 1995. **Hydrologic and erosional responses of a granitic watershed to helicopter logging and broadcast burning.** Forest Science. 41: 777-795.

Megahan, W.F.; Wilson, M.; Monsen, S.B. 2001. **Sediment production from granitic cutslopes on forest roads in Idaho, USA.** Earth Surface Processes and Landforms. 26: 153-163.

Miller, D.J.; Benda, L.E. 2000. **Effects of punctuated sediment supply on valley floor landforms and sediment transport.** Geological Society of America Bulletin. 112: 1814-1824.

Miller, E.L. 1984. **Sediment yield and storm flow response to clear cut harvest and site preparation in the Ouachita Mountains.** Water Resources Research. 20: 471-475.

Miller, E.L.; Beasley, R.S.; Lawson, E.R. 1988. **Forest harvest and site preparation effects on erosion and sedimentation in the Ouachita Mountains.** Journal of Environmental Quality. 17: 219-225.

Myers, T.; Swanson, S. 1996. **Stream morphological impact of and recovery from major flooding in north-central Nevada.** Physical Geography. 17: 431-445.

Neary, D.G.; Swift, L.W. 1987. **Rainfall thresholds for triggering a debris avalanching event in the southern Appalachian Mountains.** In: Costa, J.E.; Wieczorek, G.F., eds. Reviews in engineering geology - debris flows/avalanches: process, recognition, and mitigation. Boulder, CO: Geological Society of America: 7: 81-92.

Negishi, J.N.; Sidle, R.C.; Noguchi, S.; Nik, A.R.; Stanforth, R. 2006. **Ecological roles of roadside fern (*Dicranopteris curranii*) on logging road recovery in peninsular Malaysia: preliminary results.** Forest Ecology and Management. 224: 176-186.

Nelson, E.J.; Booth, D.B. 2002. **Sediment sources in an urbanizing, mixed land-use watershed.** Journal of Hydrology. 264: 51-68.

Patric, J.H. 1973. **Deforestation effects on soil moisture, streamflow, and water balance in the central Appalachians.** Res. Pap. NE-259. Upper Darby, PA: U.S. Department of Agriculture, Forest Service, Northeastern Forest Experiment Station. 12 p.

Patric, J.H. 1976. **Soil erosion in the eastern forest.** Journal of Forestry. 74: 671-677.

Patric, J.H. 1978. **Harvesting effects on soil and water in the eastern hardwood forest.** Southern Journal of Applied Forestry. 2: 66-73.

Patric, J.H.; Kidd, W.E.J. 1982. **Erosion on very stony forest soil during phenomenal rain in Webster County, West Virginia.** Res. Pap. NE-501. Upper Darby, PA: U.S. Department of Agriculture, Forest Service, Northeastern Forest Experiment Station. 13 p.

Patric, J.H.; Evans, J.O.; Helvey, J.D. 1984. **Summary of sediment yield data from forested land use in the United States.** Journal of Forestry. 82: 101-104.

Riverbark, B.L.; Jackson, C.R. 2004. **Concentrated flow breakthroughs moving through silvicultural streamside management zones: Southeastern Piedmont, USA.** Journal of the American Water Resources Association. 40: 1043-1052.

Robertson, G.P.; Crum, J.R.; Ellis, B.G. 1993. **The spatial variability of soil resources following long-term disturbance.** Oecologia. 96: 451-456.

Rowe, L.K.; Taylor, C.H. 1994. **Hydrology and related changes after harvesting native forest catchments and establishing *Pinus radiata* plantations. Part 3: Stream temperatures.** Hydrological Processes. 8: 299-310.

Salles, C.; Poesen, J.; Govers, G. 2000. **Statistical and physical analysis of soil detachment by raindrop impact: rain erosivity indices and threshold energy.** Water Resources Research. 36: 2721-2729.

Schmitz, M.F.; Atauri, J.A.; de Pablo, C.L.; de Agar, P.M.; Rescia, A.J.; Pineda, F.D. 1998. **Changes in land use in northern Spain: effects of forestry management on soil conservation.** Forest Ecology and Management. 109: 137-150.

Seehorn, M.E. 1985. **Stream habitat improvement handbook.** Tech. Pub. R8-TP-17. Atlanta, GA: U.S. Department of Agriculture, Forest Service, Southern Region. 27 p.

Shankman, D.; Samson, S.A. 1991. **Channelization effects on Obion River flooding, western Tennessee.** Water Resources Bulletin. 27: 247-254.

Sidle, R.C.; Ochiai, H. 2006. **Landslides: processes, prediction, and land use.** Washington, DC: American Geophysical Union. 312 p.

Sidle, R.C.; Tani, M.; Ziegler, A.D. 2006. **Catchment processes in Southeast Asia: atmospheric hydrologic, erosion, nutrient cycling, and management effects.** Forest Ecology and Management. 224: 1-4.

Sidle, R.C.; Ziegler, A.D.; Negishi, J.N.; Nik, A.R.; Siew, R.; Turkelboom, F. 2006. **Erosion processes in steep terrain - truths, myths, and uncertainties related to forest management in Southeast Asia.** Forest Ecology and Management. 224: 199-225.

Svec, J.R.; Kolka, R.K.; Stringer, J.W. 2005. **Defining perennial, intermittent, and ephemeral channels in eastern Kentucky: application to forestry best management practices.** Forest Ecology and Management. 214: 170-182.

Swift, L.W. 1984a. **Gravel and grass surfacing reduces soil loss from mountain roads.** Forest Science. 30: 657-671.

Swift, L.W. 1984b. **Soil losses from roadbeds and cut and fill slopes in the southern Appalachian Mountains.** Southern Journal of Applied Forestry. 8: 209-216.

Swift, L.W. 1986. **Filter strip widths for forest roads in the southern Appalachians.** Southern Journal of Applied Forestry. 10: 27-34.

Swift, L.W.; Burns, R.G. 1999. **The three Rs of roads: redesign, reconstruction, restoration.** Journal of Forestry. 97: 40-44.

Tague, C.; Band, L.E. 2001. **Simulating the impact of road construction and forest harvesting on hydrologic response.** Earth Surface Processes and Landforms. 26: 135-151.

Thomas, R.B.; Megahan, W.F. 1998. **Peak flow responses to clear-cutting and roads in small and large** basins, western Cascades, Oregon: a second opinion. Water Resources Research. 34: 3393-3403.

Tysdal, L.M.; Elliott, W.J.; Luce, C.H.; Black, T.A. 1999. **Modeling erosion from insloping low-volume roads with WEPP Watershed Model.** In: Proceedings of the 7th international conference on low-volume roads; 1999 May 23-26; Baton Rouge, LA. Washington, DC: National Academy Press: 2: 250-256.

VDOF. 2002. **Virginia's forestry best management practices for water quality.** 4th ed. Charlottesville, VA: Virginia Department of Forestry. 216 p.

Wahl, N.A.; Bens, O.; Schafer, B.; Huttl, R.F. 2003. **Impact of changes in land use management on soil hydrologic properties: hydraulic conductivity, water repellency, and water retention.** Physics and Chemistry of the Earth. 28: 1377-1387.

Wells, W.G. 1987. **The effects of fire on the generation of debris flows in southern California.** In: Costa, J.E.; Wieczorek, G.F., eds. Reviews in engineering geology - debris flows/avalanches: process, recognition, and mitigation. Boulder, CO: Geological Society of America: 7: 105-114.

Wemple, B.C.; Jones, J.A.; Grant, G.E. 1996. **Channel network extension by logging roads in two basins, western Cascades, Oregon.** Water Resources Bulletin. 32: 1-13.

Wieczorek, G.F. 1987. **Effect of rainfall intensity and duration on debris flows in central Santa Cruz Mountains, California.** In: Costa, J.E.; Wieczorek, G.F., eds. Reviews in engineering geology - debris flows/avalanches: process, recognition, and mitigation. Boulder, CO: Geological Society of America: 7: 93-104.

Worrell, R.; Hampson, A. 1997. **The influence of some forest operations on the sustainable management of forest soils - a review.** Forestry. 70: 61-85.

WVDOF. 2002. **Best management practices for controlling soil erosion and sedimentation from logging operations in West Virginia.** WVDOF-TR-96-3. Charleston, WV: West Virginia Department of Forestry. 29 p.

Yeakley, J.A.; Coleman, D.C.; Haines, B.L.; Kloeppel, B.D.; Meyer, J.L.; Swank, W.T.; Argo, B.W.; Deal, J.M.; Taylor, S.F. 2003. **Hillslope nutrient dynamics following upland riparian vegetation disturbance.** Ecosystems. 6: 154-167.

Ziegler, A.D.; Giambelluca, T.W.; Sutherland, R.A.; Nullet, M.A.; Yarnasarn, S.; Pinthong, J.; Preechapanya, P.; Jaiaee, S. 2004. **Toward understanding the cumulative impacts of roads in upland agricultural watersheds of northern Thailand.** Agricultural Ecosystems and Environment. 104: 145-158.

Modeling Approaches, Concepts, and Reviews

Aitken, A.P. 1973. **Assessing systematic errors in rainfall-runoff models.** Journal of Hydrology. 20: 121-136.

Andreassian, V.; Oddos, A.; Michel, C.; Anctil, F.; Perrin, C.; Loumange, C. 2004. **Impact of spatial aggregation of inputs and parameters on the efficiency of rainfall-runoff models: a theoretical study using chimera watersheds.** Water Resources Research. 40: 1-9.

Band, L.E.; Tague, C.; Groffman, P.; Belt, K. 2001. **Forest ecosystem processes at the watershed scale: hydrological and ecological controls of nitrogen export.** Hydrological Processes. 15: 2013-2028.

Beck, M.B. 1991. **Forecasting environmental change.** Journal of Forecasting. 10: 3-19.

Bencala, K.E.; Duff, J.H.; Harvey, J.W.; Jackman, A.P.; Triska, F.J. 1993. **Modelling within the stream-catchment continuum.** In: Jakeman, A.J.; et al., eds. Modelling change in environmental systems. New York: John Wiley & Sons: 163-187.

Black, P.E. 1970. **Runoff from watershed models.** Water Resources Research. 6: 465-477.

Bolstad, P.V.; Swank, W.T.; Vose, J.M. 1998. **Predicting southern Appalachian overstory vegetation with digital terrain data.** Landscape Ecology. 13: 271-283.

Bormann, H.; Diekkruger, B. 2003. **Possibilities and limitations of regional hydrological models applied within an environmental change study in Benin (West Africa).** Physics and Chemistry of the Earth. 28: 1323-1332.

Boyle, S.J.; Gupta, H.V.; Sorooshian, S.; Koren, V.; Zhang, Z.; Smith, M. 2001. **Toward improved streamflow forecasts: the value of semi-distributed modelling.** Water Resources Research. 37: 2739-2759.

Bradbrook, K.F.; Lane, S.N.; Richards, K.S. 2000. **Numerical simulation of three-dimensional, time-averaged flow structure at river channel confluences.** Water Resources Research. 36: 2731-2746.

Brath, A.; Rosso, R. 1993. **Adaptive calibration of a conceptual model for flash flood forecasting.** Water Resources Research. 29: 2561-2572.

Butts, M.B.; Payne, J.T.; Kristensen, M.; Madsen, H. 2004. **An evaluation of the impact of model structure on hydrological modelling uncertainty for streamflow simulation.** Journal of Hydrology. 298: 242-266.

Carlin, B.P.; Louis, T.A. 2000. **Bayes and empirical Bayes methods for data analysis.** 2d ed. New York: Chapman and Hall. 419 p.

Carpenter, T.M.; Georgakakos, K.P.; Sperfslagea, J.A. 2001. **On the parametric and NEXRAD-radar sensitivities of a distributed hydrologic model suitable for operational use.** Journal of Hydrology. 253: 169-193.

Chappell, N.A.; Franks, S.W.; Larenus, J. 1998. **Multi-scale permeability estimation for a tropical catchment.** Hydrological Processes. 12: 1507-1523.

Copty, N.; Rubin, Y.; Mavko, G. 1993. **Geophysical-hydrological identification of field permeability through Bayesian updating.** Water Resources Research. 29: 2813-2825.

Croke, B.F.W.; Jakeman, A.J. 2004. **A catchment moisture deficit module for the IHACRES rainfall-runoff model.** Environmental Modelling and Software. 19: 1-5.

Dietterick, B.C.; Lynch, J.A.; Corbett, E.S. 1999. **A calibration procedure using TOPMODEL to determine suitability for evaluating potential climate change effects on water yield.** Journal of the American Water Resources Division. 35: 457-468.

Duan, Q.; Gupta, H.V.; Sorooshian, S.; Rousseau, A.N.; Turcotte, R., eds. 2003. **Calibration of watershed models.** Water Sci. and Appl. Ser. Vol. 6. Washington, DC: American Geophysical Union. 346 p.

Duke, G.D.; Kienzle, S.W.; Johnson, D.L.; Byrne, J.M. 2003. **Improving overland flow routing by incorporating ancillary road data into Digital Elevation Models.** Journal of Spatial Hydrology. 3: 1-27.

Dunne, T. 1998. **Critical data requirements for prediction of erosion and sedimentation in mountain drainage basins.** Journal of the American Water Resources Association. 34: 795-808.

Dunne, T. 2001. **Problems in measuring and modeling the influence of forest management on hydrologic and geomorphic processes.** In: Wigmosta, M.S.; Burges, S.J., eds. Land use and watersheds: human influence on hydrology and geomorphology in urban and forest areas. Washington, DC: American Geophysical Union: 77-83.

Findell, K.L.; Eltahir, E.A.B. 1997. **An analysis of the soil moisture-rainfall feedback, based on direct observations from Illinois.** Water Resources Research. 33: 725-735.

Gelman, A.; Carlin, J.B.; Stern, H.S.; Rubin, D.B. 2004. **Bayesian data analysis.** 2d ed. New York: Chapman and Hall. 696 p.

Georgakakos, K.P.; Seo, D.-J.; Gupta, H.V.; Schaake, J.; Butts, M.B. 2004. **Towards the characterization of streamflow simulation uncertainty through multi-model ensembles.** Journal of Hydrology. 298: 222-241.

Govindaraju, R.S. 2000a. **Artificial neural networks in hydrology. I. Preliminary concepts.** Journal of Hydrologic Engineering. 5: 115-123.

Govindaraju, R.S. 2000b. **Artificial neural networks in hydrology. II. Hydrologic applications.** Journal of Hydrologic Engineering. 5: 124-137.

Gumbo, B.; Munyamba, N.; Sithole, G.; Savenije, H.H.G. 2002. **Coupling of digital elevation model and rainfall-runoff model in storm drainage network design.** Physics and Chemistry of the Earth. 27: 755-764.

Gupta, V.K.; Castro, S.L.; Over, T.M. 1996. **On scaling exponents of spatial peak flows from rainfall and river network geometry.** Journal of Hydrology. 187: 81-104.

Hawkins, R.H. 1975. **The importance of accurate curve numbers in the estimation of storm runoff.** Water Resources Bulletin. 11: 887-891.

He, C. 2003. **Integration of geographic information systems and simulation model for watershed management.** Environmental Modelling and Software. 18: 809-813.

Hennessy, K.J.; Gregory, J.M.; Mitchell, J.F.B. 1997. **Changes in daily precipitation under enhanced greenhouse conditions.** Climate Dynamics. 13: 667-680.

Hjelmfelt, A.T.J. 1980. **Empirical investigations of curve number technique.** Journal of the Hydraulics Division-ASCE. 106: 1471-1476.

Hodgkins, G. 1999. **Estimating the magnitude of peak flows for streams in Maine for selected recurrence intervals.** Water Resour. Invest. Rep. 99-4008. Augusta, ME: U.S. Geological Survey. 56 p.

Hooper, R.P. 2001. **Applying the scientific method to small catchment studies: a review of the Panola Mountain experience.** Hydrological Processes. 15: 2039-2050.

Islam, S.; Kothari, R. 2000. **Artificial neural networks in remote sensing of hydrologic processes.** Journal of Hydrologic Engineering. 5: 138-144.

Ivanov, V.Y.; Vivoni, E.R.; Bras, R.L.; Entekhabi, D. 2004. **Preserving high-resolution surface and rainfall data in operational-scale basin hydrology: a fully-distributed physically-based approach.** Journal of Hydrology. 298: 80-111.

Jakeman, A.J.; Littlewood, I.G.; Whitehead, P.G. 1990. **Computation of the instantaneous unit hydrograph and identifiable component flows with application to two small upland catchments.** Journal of Hydrology. 117: 275-300.

Kirkby, M.J. 1997. **TOPMODEL: a personal view.** Hydrological Processes. 11: 1087-1097.

Kite, G. 1998. **Integration of forest ecosystem and climatic models with a hydrologic model.** Journal of the American Water Resources Division. 34: 743-753.

Li, R.-H.; Simons, D.B.; Stevens, M.A. 1975. **Nonlinear kinematic wave approximation for water routing.** Water Resources Research. 11: 245-252.

Martin, J.L.; McCutcheon, S.C. 1999. **Hydrodynamics and transport for water quality modeling.** New York: Lewis. 794 p.

McCutcheon, S.C. 1989. **Water quality modeling: transport and surface exchange in rivers.** Boca Raton, FL: CRC Press. 334 p. Vol. 1.

McLaughlin, D.; Kinzelbach, W.; Ghassemi, F. 1993. **Modelling subsurface flow and transport.** In: Jakeman, A.J.; et al., eds. Modelling change in environmental systems. New York: John Wiley & Sons: 133-161.

Montanari, A.; Uhlenbrook, S. 2004. **Catchment modelling: toward an improved representation of the hydrological processes in real-world model applications.** Journal of Hydrology. 291: 159.

Newson, M.D. 1975. **Flooding and flood hazard in the United Kingdom.** Oxford, England: Oxford University Press. 60 p.

Payraudeau, S.; Tournoud, M.G.; Cernesson, F. 2003. **Sensitivity of effective rainfall amount to land use description using GIS tool - case of a small Mediterranean catchment.** Physics and Chemistry of the Earth. 28: 255-262.

Putz, G.; Burke, J.M.; Smith, D.W.; Chanasyk, D.S.; Prepas, E.E.; Mapfumo, E. 2003. **Modelling the effects of boreal forest landscape management upon streamflow and water quality: basic concepts and considerations.** Journal of Environmental Engineering and Science. 2: S87-S101.

Reed, S.; Koren, V.; Smith, M.; Zhang, Z.; Moreda, F.; Seo, D.-J.; and Distributed Model Intercomparison Proceeding (DMIP) conference participants. 2004. **Overall distributed model intercomparison results.** Journal of Hydrology. 298: 27-60.

Rosenberry, D.O.; Stannard, D.I.; Winter, T.C.; Martinez, M.L. 2004. **Comparison of 13 equations for determining evapotranspiration from a prairie wetland, Cottonwood Lake area, North Dakota, USA.** Wetlands. 24: 483-497.

Sauquet, E.; Gottschalk, L.; Leblois, E. 2000. **Mapping average annual runoff: a hierarchical approach applying a stochastic interpolation scheme.** Hydrological Sciences Journal. 45: 799-815.

Seibert, J.; Rodhe, A.; Bishop, K. 2003. **Simulating interactions between saturated and unsaturated storage in a conceptual runoff model.** Hydrological Processes. 17: 379-390.

Sidle, R.C. 2006. **Field observations and process understanding in hydrology: essential components in scaling.** Hydrological Processes. 20: 1439-1445.

Sidle, R.C.; Noguchi, S.; Tsuboyama, Y.; Laursen, K. 2001. **A conceptual model of preferential flow systems in forested hillslopes: evidence of self organization.** Hydrological Processes. 15: 1675-1692.

Singh, V.P., ed. 1995. **Computer models of watershed hydrology.** Littleton, CO: Water Resources Publications. 1144 p.

Singh, V.P.; Woolhiser, M. 2002. **Mathematical modeling of watershed hydrology.** Journal of Hydrologic Engineering. 7: 270-292.

Sivakumar, B. 2003. **Forecasting monthly streamflow dynamics in the western United States: a nonlinear dynamical approach.** Environmental Modelling and Software. 18: 721-728.

Smith, M.B.; Georgakakos, K.P.; Liang, X. 2004. **The distributed model intercomparison project (DMIP).** Journal of Hydrology. 298: 1-3.

Stewart, J.B.; Finch, J.W. 1993. **Application of remote sensing to forest hydrology.** Journal of Hydrology. 150: 701-716.

Tague, C.; Band, L.E. 2001. **Evaluating explicit and implicit routing for watershed hydro-ecological models of forest hydrology at the small catchment scale.** Hydrological Processes. 15: 1415-1439.

Thirumalaiah, K.; Deo, M.C. 2000. **Hydrological forecasting using neural networks.** Journal of Hydrologic Engineering. 5: 180-189.

Todini, E. 1988. **Rainfall-runoff modelling - past, present and future.** Journal of Hydrology. 100: 341-352.

Tokar, A.S.; Johnson, P.A. 1999. **Rainfall-runoff modelling using artificial neural networks.** Journal of Hydrologic Engineering. 4: 232-239.

Tokar, A.S.; Markus, M. 2000. **Precipitation-runoff modelling using artificial neural networks and conceptual models.** Journal of Hydrologic Engineering. 5: 156-161.

Turcotte, R.; Fortin, J.-P.; Rousseau, A.N.; Massicotte, S.; Villeneuve, J.-P. 2001. **Determination of the drainage structure of a watershed using a digital elevation model and a digital river and lake network.** Journal of Hydrology. 240: 225-242.

Uhlenbrook, S. 2003. **An empirical approach for delineating spatial units with the same dominating runoff generation processes.** Physics and Chemistry of the Earth. 28: 297-303.

Uhlenbrook, S.; Montanari, A.; de Lima, J. 2003. **Preface to the spatial issue: hydrological processes and distributed hydrological modelling.** Physics and Chemistry of the Earth. 28: 225.

Viney, N.R.; Sivapalan, M. 1996. **The hydrological response of catchments to simulated changes in climate.** Ecological Modelling. 86: 189-193.

Wagener, T.; Wheater, H.S.; Gupta, H.V. 2004. **Rainfall-runoff modelling in gauged and ungauged catchments.** Hackensack, NJ: World Scientific Publishing. 306 p.

Wheater, H.S.; Jakeman, A.J.; Beven, K.J. 1993. **Progress and directions in rainfall-runoff modeling.** In: Jakeman, A.J.; et al., eds. Modelling change in environmental systems. New York: John Wiley & Sons: 101-132.

White, E.L. 1975. **Factor analysis of drainage basin properties: classification of flood behavior in terms of basin geomorphology.** Water Resources Bulletin. 11: 676-687.

White, W.R.; Bettess, R.; Paris, E. 1982. **Analytical approach to river regime.** Journal of the Hydraulics Division-ASCE. 108: 1179-1193.

Williams, A.G.; Dowd, J.F.; Meyles, E.W. 2002. **A new interpretation of kinematic stormflow generation.** Hydrological Processes. 16: 2791-2803.

Wood, E.F.; Harley, B.M.; Perkins, F.E. 1975. **Transient flow routing in channel networks.** Water Resources Research. 11: 423-430.

Woolhiser, D.A. 1982. **Hydrologic system synthesis.** In: Haan, C.T.; Johnson, H.P.; Brakensiek, D.L., eds. Hydrologic modeling of small watersheds. St. Joseph, MI: American Society of Agricultural Engineers: 3-16.

Zecharias, Y.B.; Brutsaert, W. 1985. **Ground surface slope as a basin scale parameter.** Water Resources Research. 21: 1895-1902.

Zlotnik, V.; Ledder, G. 1993. **Groundwater velocity in an unconfined aquifer with rectangular aerial recharge.** Water Resources Research. 29: 2827-2834.

Hydrologic Model Descriptions and Application

Abbott, M.B.; Bathurst, J.C.; Cunge, J.A.; O'Connel, P.E.; Rasmussen, J. 1986a. **An introduction to the European Hydrologic System-Systeme Hydrologique Europeen. SHE. 1: History and philosophy of a physically-based, distributed modeling system.** Journal of Hydrology. 87: 45-59.

Abbott, M.B.; Bathurst, J.C.; Cunge, J.A.; O'Connel, P.E.; Rasmussen, J. 1986b. **An introduction to the European Hydrologic System-Systeme Hydrologique Europeen. SHE. 2: Structure of a physically-based, distributed modeling system.** Journal of Hydrology. 87: 61-77.

Aber, J.D.; Federer, C.A. 1992. **A generalized, lumped-parameter model of photosynthesis, evapotranspiration and net primary production in temperate and boreal forest ecosystems.** Oecologia. 92: 463-474.

Ajami, N.K.; Gupta, H.V.; Wagener, T.; Sorooshian, S. 2004. **Calibration of a semi-distributed hydrologic model for streamflow estimation along a river system.** Journal of Hydrology. 298: 112-135.

American Society of Chemical Engineers. 1996. **Hydrology handbook, ASCE manual and report on engineering practice.** 2d ed. New York: American Society of Chemical Engineers. 800 p.

Band, L.E.; Patterson, P.; Ramakrishna, N.; Running, S.W. 1993. **Forest ecosystem processes at the watershed scale: incorporating hillslope hydrology.** Agricultural and Forest Meteorology. 63: 93-126.

Bandaragoda, C.; Tarboton, D.G.; Woods, R. 2004. **Application of TOPNET in the distributed model intercomparison project.** Journal of Hydrology. 298: 178-201.

Beckers, J.; Alila, Y. 2004. **A model of rapid preferential hillslope runoff contributions to peak flow generation in a temperate rain forest watershed.** Water Resources Research. 40: W03501. Abstract. doi:10.1029/2003WR002582.

Beebe, J. 2006. **A review of integrated watershed assessment tools, non-point source models (HSPF and SWAT), and data in EPA's BASINS 3.0 and 3.1.** Tech. Bull. 913. Kalamazoo, MI: National Council for Air and Stream Improvement. 38 p.

Bowling, L.C.; Lettenmaier, D.P. 2001. **The effects of forest roads and harvest on catchment hydrology in a mountainous maritime environment.** In: Wigmosta, M.S.; Burges, S.J., eds. Land use and watersheds: human influence on hydrology and geomorphology in urban and forest areas. Washington, DC: American Geophysical Union: 145-164.

Bowling, L.C.; Storck, P.; Lettenmaier, D.P. 2000. **Hydrologic effects of logging in western Washington, United States.** Water Resources Research. 36: 3223-3240.

Campbell, K.L.; Johnson. H.P. 1975. **Hydrologic simulation of watersheds with artificial drainage.** Water Resources Research. 11: 120-126.

Carpenter, T.M.; Georgakakos, K.P. 2004. **Continuous streamflow simulation with the HRCDHM distributed hydrologic model.** Journal of Hydrology. 298: 61-79.

Chappell, N.A.; Vongtanaboon, S.; Jiang, Y.; Tangtham, N. 2006. **Return flow prediction and buffer designation in two rainforest headwaters.** Forest Ecology and Management. 224: 131-146.

Chappell, N.A.; Tych, W.; Chotai, A.; Bidin, K.; Sinun, W.; Chiew, T.H. 2006. **BARUMODEL: combined data based mechanistic models of runoff response in a managed rainforest catchment.** Forest Ecology and Management. 224: 58-80.

Chiew, F.H.S.; Stewardson, M.J.; McMahon, T.A. 1993. **Comparison of six rainfall-runoff modelling approaches.** Journal of Hydrology. 147: 1-36.

Chiu, C.-L.; Huang, J.T. 1970. **Nonlinear time varying model of rainfall-runoff relation.** Water Resources Research. 6: 1277-1286.

COE. 1998. **HEC-1 flood hydrograph package - user's manual. CPD-1A version 4.1.** Davis, CA: U.S. Army Corps of Engineers, Institute for Water Resources, Hydrologic Engineering Center. 283 p.

Cranmer, A.J.; Kouwen, N.; Mousavi, S.F. 2001. **Proving WATFLOOD: modelling the nonlinearities of hydrologic response to storm intensities.** Canadian Journal of Civil Engineering. 28: 837-855.

Croke, B.F.W.; Jakeman, A.J. 2001. **Predictions in catchment hydrology: an Australian perspective.** Marine and Freshwater Research. 52: 65-79.

Di Luzio, M. 2004. **Formulation of a hybrid calibration approach for a physically based distributed model with NEXRAD data input.** Journal of Hydrology. 298: 136-154.

Duke, G.D.; Kienzle, S.W.; Johnson, D.L.; Byrne, J.M. 2003. **Improving overland flow routing by incorporating ancillary road data into Digital Elevation Models.** Journal of Spatial Hydrology. 3: 1-27.

Dye, P.J.; Croke, B.F.W. 2003. **Evaluation of streamflow predictions by the IHACRES rainfall-runoff model in two South African catchments.** Environmental Modelling and Software. 18: 705-712.

Feldman, A.D. 1981. **HEC models for water resources system simulation: theory and experience.** Advances in Hydroscience. 12: 298-422.

Fortin, J.-P.; Turcotte, R.; Massicotte, S.; Moussa, R.; Fitzback, J.; Villeneuve, J.-P. 2001a. **Distributed watershed model compatible with remote sensing and GIS data. I: Description of model.** Journal of Hydrologic Engineering. 6: 91-99.

Fortin, J.-P.; Turcotte, R.; Massicotte, S.; Moussa, R.; Fitzback, J.; Villeneuve, J.-P. 2001b. **Distributed watershed model compatible with remote sensing and GIS data. II: Application to Chaudiere Watershed.** Journal of Hydrologic Engineering. 6: 100-108.

Frankenberger, J.R.; Brooks, E.S.; Walter, M.T.; Walter, M.F.; Steenhuis, T.A. 1999. **A GIS-based variable source area hydrology model.** Hydrological Processes. 13: 805-822.

Gerten, D.; Schaphoff, S.; Haberlandt, U.; Lucht, W.; Sitch, S. 2004. **Terrestrial vegetation and water balance - hydrological evaluation of a dynamic global vegetation model.** Journal of Hydrology. 286: 249-270.

Hawkins, R.H. 1993. **Asymptotic determination of runoff curve numbers from data.** Journal of Irrigation and Drainage Engineering-ASCE. 119: 334-345.

Hornberger, G.M.; Beven, K.J.; Cosby, B.J.; Sappington, D.E. 1985. **Shenandoah Watershed Study: calibration of a topography-based, variable contributing area hydrological model to a small forested catchment.** Water Resources Research. 21: 1841-1850.

Kirkby, M.J. 1997. **TOPMODEL: a personal view.** Hydrological Processes. 11: 1087-1097.

Ko, C.; Cheng, Q. 2004. **GIS spatial modeling of river flow and precipitation in the Oak Ridges Moraine area, Ontario.** Computers and Geosciences. 30: 379-389.

Lavigne, M.P.; Rousseau, A.N.; Turcotte, R.; Laroche, A.-M.; Fortin, J.-P.; Villeneuve, J.-P. 2004. **Validation and use of a semidistributed hydrological modelling system to predict short-term effects of clearcutting on a watershed hydrological regime.** Earth Interactions. 8: 1-19.

Lowrance, R.; Altier, L.S.; Williams, R.G.; Inamdar, S.P.; Sheridan, J.M.; Bosch, D.D.; Hubbard, R.K.; Thomas, D.L. 2000. **REMM: the riparian ecosystem management model.** Journal of Soil and Water Conservation. 55: 27-34.

Mbajiorgu, C.C. 1995a. **Watershed resources management (WRM) model. 1: Model description.** Computers and Electronics in Agriculture. 13: 195-216.

Mbajiorgu, C.C. 1995b. **Watershed resources management (WRM) model. 2: An application to the Upper Wilmot Watershed.** Computers and Electronics in Agriculture. 13: 217-226.

Mockus, V. 1972. **Estimation of direct runoff from storm rainfall.** SCS National Engineering Handbook, Section 4, Chapter 10. Washington, DC: Soil Conservation Service: 10.1-10.24.

NCASI. 2003. **Technical documentation for SED-MODL version 2.0.** National Council for Air and Stream Improvement, Inc. [Available on line: http://www.ncasi.org/support/downloads/default.aspx?id=5. (March 10, 2007)]

Olsen, J.R.; Beling, P.A.; Lambert, J.H. 2000. **Dynamic models for floodplain management.** Journal of Water Resources Planning and Management-ASCE. 126: 167-175.

Rajurkar, M.P.; Kothyari, U.C.; Chaube, U.C. 2004. **Modeling of the daily rainfall-runoff relationship with artificial neural network.** Journal of Hydrology. 285: 96-113.

Rousseau, A.N.; Mailhot, A.; Rucotte, R.; Duchemin, M.; Blachette, C.; Roux, M.; Etong, N.; Dupont, J.; Villeneuve, J.-P. 2000. **GIBSI - an integrated modelling system prototype for river basin management.** Hydrobiologia. 422/423: 465-475.

Scanlon, T.M.; Raffensperger, J.P.; Hornberger, G.M.; Clapp, R.B. 2000. **Shallow subsurface storm flow in a forested headwater catchment: observations and modeling using a modified TOPMODEL.** Water Resources Research. 36: 2575-2586.

Singh, V.P.; Frevert, D.K., eds. 2002. **Mathematical models of large watershed hydrology.** Highlands Ranch, CO: Water Resources Publications. 891 p.

Singh, V.P.; Frevert, D.K., eds. 2002b. **Mathematical models of small watershed hydrology and applications.** Highlands Ranch. CO: Water Resources Publications. 972 p.

Sivertun, A.; Prange, L. 2003. **Non-point source critical area analysis in the Gisselo watershed using GIS.** Environmental Modelling and Software. 18: 887-898.

Storck, P.; Bowling, L.C.; Wetherbee, P.; Lettenmaier, D.P. 1998. **Application of a GIS-based distributed hydrology model for prediction of forest harvest effects on peak stream flow in the Pacific Northwest.** Hydrological Processes. 12: 889-904.

Svoboda, A. 1991. **Changes in flood regime by use of the modified curve number method.** Hydrological Sciences Journal. 36: 461-470.

Tague, C.; Band, L.E. 2001. **Simulating the impact of road construction and forest harvesting on hydrologic response.** Earth Surface Processes and Landforms. 26: 135-151.

Tysdal, L.M.; Elliott, W.J.; Luce, C.H.; Black, T.A. 1999. **Modeling erosion from insloping low-volume roads with WEPP Watershed Model.** In: Proceedings of 7th international conference on low-volume roads; 1999 May 23-26; Baton Rouge, LA. Washington, DC: National Academy Press: 2: 250-256.

Vertessy, R.A.; Hatton, T.J.; O'Shaughnessy, P.J.; Jayasuriya, M.D. 1993. **Predicting water yield from a mountain ash forest catchment using a terrain analysis based catchment model.** Journal of Hydrology. 150: 665-700.

Walter, M.T.; Mehta, V.K.; Marrone, A.M.; Boll, J.; Gerard-Marchant, P.; Steenhuis, T.S.; Walter, M.F. 2003. **Simple estimation of prevalence of Hortonian flow in New York City watersheds.** Journal of Hydrologic Engineering. 8: 214-218.

White, I.; Broadbridge, P. 1988. **Constant rate rainfall infiltration: a versatile nonlinear model. 2. Application of solutions.** Water Resources Research. 24: 155-162.

Wigmosta, M.S.; Perkins, W.A. 2001. **Simulating the effects of forest roads on watershed hydrology.** In: Wigmosta, M.S.; Burges, S.J., eds. Land use and watersheds: human influence on hydrology and geomorphology in urban and forest areas. Washington, DC: American Geophysical Union: 127-143.

Wigmosta, M.S.; Vail, L.W.; Lettenmaier, D.P. 1994. **A distributed hydrology-vegetation model for complex terrain.** Water Resources Research. 30: 1665-1679.

Yarnal, B.; Lakhtakia, M.N.; Yu, Z.; White, R.A.; Pollard, D.; Miller, D.A.; Lapenta, W.M. 2000. **A linked meteorological and hydrological model system: the Susquehanna River Basin Experiment (SRBEX).** Global and Planetary Change. 25: 149-161.

Ye, W.; Bates, B.C.; Viney, N.R.; Sivapalan, M. 1997. **Performance of conceptual rainfall-runoff models in low-yielding ephemeral catchments.** Water Resources Research. 33: 153-166.

Zhu, Z.; Arp, P.; Meng, F.; Bourque, C.; Foster, N. 2003. **A forest nutrient and biomass model (ForNBM) based on year-round, monthly weather conditions. Part I: Assumption, structure and processing.** Ecological Modelling. 169: 347-360.

Land Use Hydrologic Modeling

Bhaduri, B.; Harbor, J.; Engel, B.A.; Grove, M. 2000. **Assessing watershed-scale, long-term hydrologic impacts of land-use change using a GIS-NPS model.** Environmental Management. 26: 643-658.

Bhaduri, B.; Minner, M.; Tatalovich, S.; Harbor, J. 2001. **Long-term hydrologic impact of urbanization: a tale of two models.** Journal of Water Resources Planning and Management-ASCE. 127: 13-19.

Boyle, S.J.; Tsanis, I.K.; Kanaroglou, P.S. 1998. **Developing geographic information systems for land use impact assessment in flooding conditions.** Journal of Water Resources Planning and Management-ASCE. 124: 89-98.

Coulthard, T.J.; Kirkby, M.J.; Macklin, M.G. 2000. **Modelling geomorphic response to environmental change in an upland catchment.** Hydrological Processes. 14: 2031-2045.

De Roo, A.; Schmuck, G.; Perdigao, V.; Thielen, J. 2003. **The influence of historic land use changes and future planned land use scenarios on floods in the Oder catchment.** Physics and Chemistry of the Earth. 28: 1291-1300.

Engel, B.A.; Choi, J.-Y.; Harbor, J.; Pandey, S. 2003. **Web-based DSS for hydrologic impact evaluation of small watershed land use changes.** Computers and Electronics in Agriculture. 39: 241-249.

Fohrer, N.; Moller, D.; Steiner, N. 2002. **An interdisciplinary modelling approach to evaluate the effects** of land use change. Physics and Chemistry of the Earth. 27: 655-662.

Helmschrot, J.; Flugel, W.-A. 2002. **Land use characterisation and change detection analysis for hydrological model parameterisation of large scale afforested areas using remote sensing.** Physics and Chemistry of the Earth. 27: 711-718.

Kepner, W.G.; Semmems, D.J.; Bassett, S.D.; Mouat, D.A.; Goodrich, D.C. 2004. **Scenario analysis for the San Pedro River, analyzing hydrological consequences of a future environment.** Environmental Monitoring and Assessment. 94: 115-127.

Klocking, B.; Haberlandt, U. 2002. **Impact of land use changes on water dynamics - a case study in temperate meso and macroscale river basins.** Physics and Chemistry of the Earth. 27: 619-629.

Krause, P. 2002. **Quantifying the impact of land use changes on the water balance of large catchments using the J2000 model.** Physics and Chemistry of the Earth. 27: 663-673.

Kuczera, G.; Raper, G.P.; Brah, N.S.; Jayasuriya, M.D. 1993. **Modelling yield changes after strip thinning in a mountain ash catchment: an exercise in catchment model validation.** Journal of Hydrology. 150: 433-457.

Ludwig, R.; Probeck, M.; Mauser, W. 2003. **Mesoscale water balance modelling in the Upper Danube watershed using sub-scale land cover information derived from NOAA-AVHRR imagery and GIS-techniques.** Physics and Chemistry of the Earth. 28: 1351-1364.

Molders, N.; Ruhaak, W. 2002. **On the impact of explicitly predicted runoff on the simulated atmospheric response to small-scale land-use changes: an integrated modelling approach.** Atmospheric Research. 63: 3-38.

Niehoff, D.; Fritsch, U.; Bronstert, A. 2002. **Land-use impacts on storm-runoff generation: scenarios of** land-use change and simulation of hydrological response in a meso-scale catchment in SW-Germany. Journal of Hydrology 267: 80-93.

Pauleit, S.; Duhme, F. 2000. **Assessing the environmental performance of land cover types for urban planning.** Landscape and Urban Planning. 52: 1-20.

Rodriguez, F.; Andrieu, H.; Zech, Y. 2000. **Evaluation of a distributed model for urban catchments using a 7-year continuous data series.** Hydrological Processes. 14: 899-914.

Schoorl, J.M.: Veldkamp, A. 2001. **Linking land use and landscape process modelling: a case study for the Alora Region (south Spain).** Agricultural Ecosystems and Environment. 85: 281-292.

Wegehenkle, M. 2002. **Estimating of the impact of land use changes using the conceptual hydrological model THESEUS - a case study.** Physics and Chemistry of the Earth. 27: 631-640.

Wegehenkle, M. 2003. **Long-term evaluation of land use changes on catchment water balance - a case study from North-East Germany.** Physics and Chemistry of the Earth. 28: 1281-1290.

Weng, Q. 2001. **Modeling urban growth effects on surface runoff with the integration of remote sensing and GIS.** Environmental Management. 28: 737-748.

Wooldridge, S.; Kalma, J.; Kuczera, G. 2001. **Parameterisation of a simple semi-distributed model for assessing the impact of land-use on hydrologic response.** Journal of Hydrology. 254: 16-32.

Hillslope Hydrologic Modeling

Aryal, S.K.; Mein, R.G.; O'Loughlin, E.M. 2002. **The concept of effective length in hillslopes: assessing the influence of climate and topography on the contributing areas of catchments.** Hydrological Processes. 17: 131-151.

Band, L.E.; Patterson, P.; Ramakrishna, N.; Running, S.W. 1993. **Forest ecosystem processes at the watershed scale: incorporating hillslope hydrology.** Agricultural and Forest Meteorology. 63: 93-126.

Band, L.E.; Tague, C.; Groffman, P.; Belt, K. 2001. **Forest ecosystem processes at the watershed scale: hydrological and ecological controls of nitrogen export.** Hydrological Processes. 15: 2013-2028.

Binley, A.; Beven, K.L. 1992. **Three-dimensional modelling of hillslope hydrology.** Hydrological Processes. 6: 347-359.

Brandes, D.; Duffy, C.J.; Cusumano, J.P. 1998. **Stability and damping in a dynamical model of hillslope hydrology.** Water Resources Research. 34: 3303-3313.

Bronstert, A. 1999. **Capabilities and limitations of detailed hillslope hydrological modelling.** Hydrological Processes. 13: 21-48.

Cloke, H.L.; Renaud, J.-P.; Claxton, A.J.; McDonnell, J.J.; Anderson, M.G.; Blake, J.R.; Bates, P.D. 2003. **The effect of model configuration on modelled hillslope-riparian interactions.** Journal of Hydrology. 279: 167-181.

Flugel, W.-A.; Smith, R.E. 1999. **Integrated process studies and modelling simulations of hillslope hydrology and interflow dynamics using the HILLS model.** Environmental Modelling and Software. 14: 153-160.

Hilberts, A.G.J.; van Loon, E.E.; Troch, P.A.; Paniconi, C. 2004. **The hillslope-storage Boussinesq model for non-constant bedrock slope.** Journal of Hydrology. 291: 160-173.

Jones, J.A.; Connelly, L.J. 2002. **A semi-distributed simulation model for natural pipeflow.** Journal of Hydrology. 262: 28-49.

Keim, R.F.; Skaugset, A.E. 2003. **Modelling effects of forest canopies on slope stability.** Hydrological Processes. 17: 1457-1467.

Kirkby, M.J. 1988. **Hillslope runoff processes and models.** Journal of Hydrology. 100: 315-339.

Kosugi, K.; Uchida, T.; Mizuyama, T. 2004. **Numerical calculation of soil pipe flow and its effect on water dynamics in a slope.** Hydrological Processes. 18: 777-789.

McLaughlin, D.; Kinzelbach, W.; Ghassemi, F. 1993. **Modelling subsurface flow and transport.** In: Jakeman, A.J.; et al., eds. Modelling change in environmental systems. New York: John Wiley & Sons: 133-161.

Weiler, M.; McDonnell, J.J. 2004. **Virtual experiments: a new approach for improving process conceptualization in hillslope hydrology.** Journal of Hydrology. 285: 3-18.

Modeling Issues

Addicott, J.F.; Aho, J.M.; Antolin, M.F.; Padilla, D.K.; Richardson, J.S.; Soluk, D.A. 1987. **Ecological neighborhoods: scaling environmental patterns.** Oikos. 49: 340-346.

Aitken, A.P. 1973. **Assessing systematic errors in rainfall-runoff models.** Journal of Hydrology. 20: 121-136.

Band, L.E. 1993. **Effect of land surface representation on forest water and carbon budgets.** Journal of Hydrology. 150: 749-772.

Bartolini, P.; Salas, J.D. 1993. **Modeling of streamflow processes at different time scales.** Water Resources Research. 29: 2573-2587.

Benda, L.E.; Andras, K.; Miller, D.; Bigelow, P. 2004. **Confluence effects in rivers: interactions of basin scale, network geometry, and disturbance regimes.** Water Resources Research. 40: 1-15.

Beven, K.J.; Wood, E.F.; Sivapalan, M. 1988. **On hydrologic heterogeneity - catchment morphology and catchment response.** Journal of Hydrology. 100: 353-375.

Black, P.E. 1972. **Hydrograph responses to geomorphic model watershed characteristics and precipitation variables.** Journal of Hydrology. 17: 309-329.

Bonell, M. 1993. **Progress in the understanding of runoff generation dynamics in forests.** Journal of Hydrology. 150: 217-275.

Bonell, M. 1998. **Selected challenges in runoff generation research in forests from the hillslope to headwater drainage basin scale.** Journal of the American Water Resources Division. 34: 765-785.

Bongartz, K. 2003. **Applying different spatial distribution and modelling concepts in three nested mesoscale catchments of Germany.** Physics and Chemistry of the Earth. 28: 1343-1349.

Booij, M.J. 2003. **Determination and integration of appropriate spatial scales for river basin modelling.** Hydrological Processes. 17: 2581-2598.

Brath, A.; Montanari, A. 2003. **Sensitivity of the peak flows to the spatial variability of the soil infiltration capacity for different climatic scenarios.** Physics and Chemistry of the Earth. 28: 247-254.

Bren, L.J. 1998. **The geometry of a constant buffer-loading design method for humid watersheds.** Forest Ecology and Management. 110: 113-125.

Bronstert, A.; Bardossy, A. 2003. **Uncertainty of runoff modelling at the hillslope scale due to temporal variations of rainfall intensity.** Physics and Chemistry of the Earth. 28: 283-288.

Butts, M.B.; Payne, J.T.; Kristensen, M.; Madsen, H. 2004. **An evaluation of the impact of model structure on hydrological modelling uncertainty for streamflow simulation.** Journal of Hydrology. 298: 242-266.

Carpenter, T.M.; Georgakakos, K.P. 2004. **Impacts of parametric and radar rainfall uncertainty on the ensemble streamflow simulations of a distributed hydrologic model.** Journal of Hydrology. 298: 202-221.

Chappell, N.A.; Franks, S.W.; Larenus, J. 1998. **Multi-scale permeability estimation for a tropical catchment.** Hydrological Processes. 12: 1507-1523.

De Lima, J.; Singh, V.P. 2003. **Laboratory experiments on the influence of storm movement on overland flow.** Physics and Chemistry of the Earth. 28: 277-282.

Duke, G.D.; Kienzle, S.W.; Johnson, D.L.; Byrne, J.M. 2003. **Improving overland flow routing by incorporating ancillary road data into Digital Elevation Models.** Journal of Spatial Hydrology. 3: 1-27.

Dutilleul, P.; Legendre, P. 1993. **Spatial heterogeneity against heteroscedasticity: an ecological paradigm versus a statistical concept.** Oikos. 66: 152-171.

Ehrenfeld, J.G.; Han, X.; Parsons, W.F.J.; Zhu, W. 1997. **On the nature of environmental gradients: temporal and spatial variability of soils and vegetation in the New Jersey Pinelands.** Ecology. 85: 785-798.

Fohrer, N. 2003. **Recent developments in river basin research and management.** Physics and Chemistry of the Earth. 28: 1279.

Georgakakos, K.P.; Seo, D.-J.; Gupta, H.V.; Schaake, J.; Butts, M.B. 2004. **Towards the characterization of streamflow simulation uncertainty through multi-model ensembles.** Journal of Hydrology. 298: 222-241.

Giannoni, F.; Roth, G.; Rudari, R. 2003. **Can the behavior of different basins be described by the same model's parameter set? A geomorphologic framework.** Physics and Chemistry of the Earth. 28: 289-295.

Guo, J.; Liang, X.; Leung, L.R. 2004. **Impacts of different precipitation data sources on water budgets.** Journal of Hydrology. 298: 11-334.

Hawkins, R.H. 1975. **The importance of accurate curve numbers in the estimation of storm runoff.** Water Resources Bulletin. 11: 887-891.

Hawkins, R.H. 1993. **Asymptotic determination of runoff curve numbers from data.** Journal of Irrigation and Drainage Engineering-ASCE. 119: 334-345.

Herbst, M.; Diekkruger, B. 2002. **The influence of the spatial structure of soil properties on water balance modeling in a microscale catchment.** Physics and Chemistry of the Earth. 27: 701-710.

Herbst, M.; Diekkruger, B. 2003. **Modelling the spatial variability of soil moisture in a micro-scale catchment and comparison with field data using geostatistics.** Physics and Chemistry of the Earth. 28: 239-245.

Hjelmfelt, A.T.J. 1980. **Empirical investigations of curve number technique.** Journal of the Hydraulics Division-ASCE. 106: 1471-1476.

Hooper, R.P. 2001. **Applying the scientific method to small catchment studies: a review of the Panola Mountain experience.** Hydrological Processes. 15: 2039-2050.

Hoosbeek, M.R.; Bryant, R.B. 1992. **Toward the quantitative modeling of pedogenesis - a review.** Geoderma. 55: 183-210.

Hornbeck, J.W. 1973. **The problem of extreme events in paired-watershed studies.** Res. Note NE-175. Upper Darby, PA: U.S. Department of Agriculture, Forest Service, Northeastern Forest Experiment Station. 4 p.

Jakeman, A.J.; Hornberger, G.M. 1993. **How much complexity is warranted in a rainfall-runoff model?** Water Resources Research. 29: 2637-2649.

Lee, R. 1970. **Theoretical estimates versus forest water yield.** Water Resources Research. 6: 1327-1334.

Lenhart, T.; Eckhardt, K.; Fohrer, N.; Frede, H.-G. 2002. **Comparison of two different approaches of sensitivity analysis.** Physics and Chemistry of the Earth. 27: 645-654.

Levin, S.A. 1992. **The problem of pattern and scale in ecology.** Ecology. 73: 1943-1967.

Li, H.; Reynolds, R.F. 1995. **On definition and quantification of heterogeneity.** Oikos. 73: 280-284.

Liang, X.; Guo, J.; Leung, L.R. 2004. **Assessment of the effects of spatial resolutions on daily water flux simulations.** Journal of Hydrology. 298: 287-310.

McCulloch, J.; Robinson, M. 1993. **History of forest hydrology.** Journal of Hydrology. 150: 189-216.

McDonnell, J.J. 2005. **Discussion of "Simple estimation of prevalence of Hortonian flow in New York City watersheds."** Journal of Hydrologic Engineering. 10: 168-169.

Moore, I.D.; Lewis, A.; Gallant, J.C. 1993. **Terrain attributes: estimation methods and scale effects.** In: Jakeman, A.J.; et al., eds. Modelling change in environmental systems. New York: John Wiley & Sons: 189-214.

Moore, I.D.; Norton, T.W.; Williams, J.E. 1993. **Modelling environmental heterogeneity in forested landscapes.** Journal of Hydrology. 150: 717-747.

Morton, A. 1993. **Mathematical models: questions of trustworthiness.** British Journal of the Philosophy of Science. 44: 659-674.

Muradian, R. 2001. **Ecological thresholds: a survey.** Ecological Economics. 38: 7-24.

Newson, M.D. 1975. **Flooding and flood hazard in the United Kingdom.** Oxford, England: Oxford University Press. 60 p.

Ogden, F.L.; Julien, P.Y. 1993. **Runoff sensitivity to temporal and spatial rainfall variability at runoff plane and small basin scales.** Water Resources Research. 29: 2589-2597.

Overton, D.E. 1970. **Route or convolute?** Water Resources Research. 6: 43-52.

Pickett, S.T.A.; Cadenasso, M.L. 1995. **Landscape ecology: spatial heterogeneity in ecological systems.** Science. 269: 331-334.

Poff, N.L. 1996. **A hydrogeography of unregulated streams in the United States and an examination of scale-dependence in some hydrological descriptors.** Freshwater Biology. 36: 71-91.

Robertson, G.P.; Crum, J.R.; Ellis, B.G. 1993. **The spatial variability of soil resources following long-term disturbance.** Oecologia. 96: 451-456.

Robinson, J.S.; Sivapalan, M. 1997. **An investigation into the physical causes of scaling and heterogeneity of regional flood frequency.** Water Resources Research. 33: 1045-1059.

Ryan, P.J.; McKenzie, N.J.; O'Connel, D.O.; Loughhead, A.N.; Leppert, P.M.; Jacquier, D.; Ashton, L. 2000. **Integrating forest soils information across scales: spatial prediction of soil properties under Australian forests.** Forest Ecology and Management. 138: 139-157.

Sidle, R.C. 2006. **Field observations and process understanding in hydrology: essential components in scaling.** Hydrological Processes. 20: 1439-1445.

Sidle, R.C.; Tsuboyama, Y.; Noguchi, S.; Hosoda, I.; Fujieda, M.; Shimizu, T. 1995. **Seasonal hydrologic response at various spatial scales in a small forested catchment, Hitachi Ohta, Japan.** Journal of Hydrology. 168: 227-250.

Smith, J.A. 1992. **Representation of basin scale in flood peak distributions.** Water Resources Research. 28: 2993-2999.

Smith, M.B.; Koren, V.; Zhang, Z.; Reed, S.; Pan, J.-J.; Moreda, F. 2004. **Runoff response to spatial variability in precipitation: an analysis of observed data.** Journal of Hydrology. 298: 267-286.

Torres, R. 2002. **A threshold condition for soil-water transport.** Hydrological Processes. 16: 2703-2706.

Torres, R.; Alexander, L.J. 2002. **Intensity-duration effects on drainage: column experiments at near-zero pressure head.** Water Resources Research. 38: 1-10.

Waring, R.H.; Running, S.W. 1998. **Forest ecosystem: analysis at multiple scales.** 2d ed. San Diego, CA: Academic Press. 370 p.

Weins, J.A. 2000. **Ecological heterogeneity: an ontogeny of concepts and approaches.** In: Hutchings, M.J.; John, E.A.; Stewart, A.J.A., eds. The ecological consequences of environmental heterogeneity. Malden, MA: Blackwell Science: 9-32.

Wilson, C.B.; Valdes, J.B.; Rodrigues-Iturbe, I. 1979. **On the influence of the spatial distribution of rainfall on storm runoff.** Water Resources Research. 15: 321-328.

Winchell, M.; Gupta, H.V.; Sorooshian, S. 1998. **On the simulation of infiltration- and saturation-excess runoff using radar-based rainfall estimates: effects of algorithm uncertainty and pixel aggregation.** Water Resources Research. 34: 2655-2670.

Wood, E.F.; Sivapalan, M.; Beaven, K. 1990. **Similarity and scale in catchment storm response.** Reviews of Geophysics. 28: 1-18.

Flood Frequency Analysis

Brissette, F.P.; Leconte, R.; Marche, C.; Rousselle, J. 2003. **Historical evolution of flooding damage on a USA/Quebec River Basin.** Journal of the American Water Resources Association. 39: 1385-1396.

Burn, D.H.; Goel, N.K. 2000. **The formation of groups for regional flood frequency analysis.** Hydrological Sciences Journal. 45: 97-112.

Corradini, C.; Morbidelli, R.; Saltalippi, C.; Melone, F. 2004. **Flood forecasting and infiltration modelling.** Hydrological Sciences Journal. 49: 277-236.

Crippen, J.R. 1982. **Envelope curves for extreme flood events.** Journal of the Hydraulics Division-ASCE. 108: 1208-1212.

Crippen, J.R.; Bue, C.D. 1977. **Maximum floodflows in the conterminous United States.** Water-Supply Pap. 1887. Washington, DC: U.S. Geological Survey. 52 p.

Cunnane, C. 1988. **Methods and merits of regional flood frequency analysis.** Journal of Hydrology. 100: 269-290.

Davidson, A.C.; Smith, R.L. 1990. **Models for exceedances over high thresholds.** Journal of the Royal Statistical Society, Series B (Methodological). 52: 393-442.

Giordano, L.A.; Fritsch, J.M. 1991. **Strong tornados and flash-flood-producing rainstorms during the warm season in the Mid-Atlantic Region.** Weather and Forecasting. 6: 437-455.

Graybeal, D.Y.; Leathers, D.L. 2006. **Snowmelt-related flood risk in Appalachia: first estimates from historical snow climatology.** Journal of Applied Meteorology and Climatology. 45: 178-193.

Gupta, V.K.; Castro, S.L.; Over, T.M. 1996. **On scaling exponents of spatial peak flows from rainfall and river network geometry.** Journal of Hydrology. 187: 81-104.

Hollis, G.E. 1975. **The effect of urbanization on floods of different recurrence interval.** Water Resources Research. 11: 431-435.

Hosking, J.R.M.; Wallis, J.R.; Wood, E.F. 1985. **An appraisal of the regional flood frequency procedure in the UK.** Hydrological Sciences Journal. 30: 85-109.

IACWD. 1982. **Guidelines for determining flood flow frequency.** Bull. 17B. Reston, VA: U.S. Geological Survey, Interagency Advisory Committee on Water Data. 186 p.

Javelle, P.; Ouarda, T.; Lang, M.; Bobee, B.; Galea, G.; Gresillon, J. 2002. **Development of regional flood-duration-frequency curves based on the index-flood method.** Journal of Hydrology. 258: 249-259.

Kite, G.W. 1975. **Confidence limits for design events.** Water Resources Research. 11: 48-53.

Kunkel, K.E.; Andsager, K.; Easterling, D.R. 1999. **Long-term trends in extreme precipitation events over the conterminous United States and Canada.** Journal of Climate. 12: 2515-2527.

Lecce, S.A. 2000. **Spatial variations in the timing of annual floods in the southeastern United States.** Journal of Hydrology. 235: 151-169.

Madsen, H.; Rosbjerg, D. 1997a. **The partial duration series method in regional index-flood modeling.** Water Resources Research. 33: 737-746.

Madsen, H.; Rosbjerg, D. 1997b. **Generalized least squares and empirical Bayes estimation in regional partial duration series index-flood modeling.** Water Resources Research. 33: 771-781.

Madsen, H.; Pearson, C.P.; Rosbjerg, D. 1997. **Comparison of annual maximum series and partial duration series methods for modelling extreme hydrologic events. 2. Regional modeling.** Water Resources Research. 33: 759-769.

Madsen, H.; Rasmussen, P.F.; Rosbjerg, D. 1997. **Comparison of annual maximum series and partial duration series methods for modelling extreme hydrologic events. 1. At-site modeling.** Water Resources Research. 33: 747-757.

McCuen, R.H.; Beighley, R.E. 2003. **Seasonal flow frequency analysis.** Journal of Hydrology. 279: 43-56.

Morrison, J.E.; Smith, J.A. 2002. **Stochastic modeling of flood peaks using the generalized extreme value distribution.** Water Resources Research. 38: 1305. WR000502. Abstract. doi:10.1029/2001WR000502.

Newson, M.D. 1975. **Flooding and flood hazard in the United Kingdom.** Oxford, England: Oxford University Press. 60 p.

Potter, K.W. 1987. **Research on flood frequency analysis: 1983-1983.** Reviews of Geophysics. 25: 113-118.

Reed, S.; Johnson, D.; Sweeney, T. 2002. **Application and national geographic information system database to support two-year flood and threshold runoff estimates.** Journal of Hydrologic Engineering. 7: 209-219.

Reich, B.M. 1970. **Flood series compared to rainfall extremes.** Water Resources Research. 6: 1655-1667.

Reis, K.G.I.; Crouse, M.Y. 1992. **The national flood frequency program, Version 3.** Water Resour. Invest. Rep. 02-4168. Reston, VA: U.S. Geological Survey. 53 p.

Robinson, J.S.; Sivapalan, M. 1997. **An investigation into the physical causes of scaling and heterogeneity of regional flood frequency.** Water Resources Research. 33: 1045-1059.

Sauquet, E.; Gottschalk, L.; Leblois, E. 2000. **Mapping average annual runoff: a hierarchical approach applying a stochastic interpolation scheme.** Hydrological Sciences Journal. 45: 799-815.

Smith, J.A. 1992. **Representation of basin scale in flood peak distributions.** Water Resources Research. 28: 2993-2999.

Stedinger, J.R.; Baker, V.R. 1987. **Surface water hydrology: historical and paleoflood information.** Reviews of Geophysics. 25: 119-124.

Stedinger, J.R.; Vogel, R.M.; Foufoula-Georgiou, E. 1993. **Frequency analysis of extreme events.** In: Maidment, D.R., ed. Handbook of hydrology. New York: McGraw-Hill: 18.1-18.66.

Sturdevant-Rees, P.; Smith, J.A.; Morrison, J.E.; Baeck, M.L. 2001. **Tropical storms and the flood hydrology of the central Appalachians.** Water Resources Research. 37: 2143-2168.

Thomas, W.O.; Kirby, W.H. 2002. **Estimation of extreme floods.** In: Ries, K.G.; Crouse, M.Y., eds. The national flood frequency program, Version 3. Water Resour. Invest. Rep. 02-4168. Reston, VA: U.S. Geological Survey: 12-14.

Troch, P.A.; Smith, C.T.; Wood, E.F.; DeTroch, F.P. 1994. **Hydrologic controls of large floods in a small basin: central Appalachian case study.** Journal of Hydrology. 156: 285-309.

GPO U.S. GOVERNMENT PRINTING OFFICE: 2007—645-325/60005